AN

INDIAN JOURNALIST

AN

INDIAN JOURNALIST

BEING THE

LIFE, LETTERS AND CORRESPONDENCE

OF

DR. SAMBHU C. MOOKERJEE

F. H. SKRINE, I. C. S.

GYAN

Published by

GYAN

Gyan Publishing House
5, Ansari Road
Daryaganj, New Delhi-110002
Phone: 011-47034999, 9811692060
E-mail: books@gyanbooks.com

Distribution Network
gyanbooks.com
India, USA, Canada, UK, Australia, France

ISBN: 978-81-212-8973-3 (PB)
First Published, 1895

2nd Impression 2023

Printed at: Gyan Press, Delhi.

AN INDIAN JOURNALIST

AUTHOR: DR. SAMBHU C. MOOKERJEE, F. H. SKRINE

AN

INDIAN JOURNALIST:

BEING THE

LIFE, LETTERS AND CORRESPONDENCE

OF

DR. SAMBHU C. MOOKERJEE

LATE EDITOR OF 'REIS AND RAYYET'
CALCUTTA.

BY

F. H. SKRINE, I.C.S.

Calcutta:

THACKER, SPINK & CO.

1895.

INDEX.

DEDICATION.

DEDICATION.

United Service Club,

Calcutta, the 2nd September, 1895.

MY DEAR HUNTER,

IF, as the Greeks said, a huge book is a huge evil, a lengthy preface is a greater one. Mine, therefore, shall have the merit of brevity. Gratitude was amongst the motives which led me to undertake the biography of my distinguished Bengali friend ; for he gave me sympathy and kindness at a time when I stood in need of both. I felt, too, that his career was one which should not be allowed to pass into oblivion. He came of a race which has undergone presistent vituperation from people forgetful of Burke's aphorism that a nation may not be impeached. The detractors of the Bengalis belong to two classes. The first know nothing of the seventy millions of the Lower Provinces ; and have been dazzled by the brilliant sophistries of

Macaulay. The second judge Bengalis, as Macaulay did, by the cringing sycophants who dance attendance in high officials' anterooms or belong to families who, during a century of intercourse with us in the capital, have lost some of their native virtues without acquiring ours. It is a remarkable fact that one seldom finds this attitude of contempt in Englishmen who are intimately acquainted with the Bengali language and character. The Bengalis have their faults, and serious ones. A want of moral courage is the chief one. Most of their failings, however, are due to defective education—an absence of healthy home life and of the thorough training for thews and sinews which English lads enjoy. Bengalis who have been vouchsafed such advantages compare not unfavourably with the average Englishman. Mookerjee was an instance of a Bengali with "backbone"—from what ancestral strain derived I know not. The story of his life, told with its shadows as well as its lights, is pregnant with lessons for us all. There is a peculiar fitness in the association of your name with this narrative. I commenced it at your beautiful Berkshire home. Well do I remember how, while viewing thence the wide stretch of woodlands and pasture over which the spirit of our Saxon Alfred still seems to hover, I thought that the fortunes of the much-maligned Bengalis might have been far different if their annals had included a name such as his. The life of a nation is inspired and sustained by the examples of its great men. The subject of this biography was prompt to recognize your genius, and his review of its first fruits, the *Annals of Rural Bengal*, was sympathetic and appreciative. I cannot but be grateful for the permission accorded me to dedicate my little book to you.

Believe me,

Your's sincerely,

F. H. SKRINE.

SIR W. W. HUNTER, K.C.S.I., C.I.E., &C., &C.,

Oaken Holt, Cumnor.

HIS LIFE STORY.

HIS LIFE STORY.

THERE is something inexpressibly touching in the eagerness with which we strive to rend the veil concealing the personality of distinguished men. We love to see them in dishabille, so to speak: to know their inmost thoughts, the trivial incidents of their daily lives. No biographers retain a lasting hold on the public taste but those who gratify this universal passion. Like all our sentiments it is based on mixed motives. Curiosity is among them: but there is also a secret desire to compare our own sensations and impulses with those of our hero. And in contemplating the weaknesses besetting the noblest natures we are consoled for our own, as a token of the kinship which binds together all human beings. Emerson notes this deep-seated instinct. "Great geniuses," he says, "have the shortest biographies. Their cousins can tell you nothing about them. They live in their writings. And so their home and school life are trivial and commonplace. If you would know their tastes and complexions, the most admiring of their readers most resemble them." This dictum, *pace tanti viri*, is wanting in truth as well as in originality. Men of the highest intellect are not gregarious. A craving for intercourse with others comes of a vacant mind: and the little knot who, in every age, hold high the lamp of progress shun the babble of the common herd. The world, wrote one of them, has never given me anything so good but that, in probing the depths of my own nature, I have found something far better there. Those outpourings of soul in which a faithful biographer rejoices are never indulged in by men who have acquired the reverence of their fellows. There are natures as pure, as dazzling, and as inaccessible as the highest peaks of the Himalayas: and not material for their life-story but a historian capable of assimilating it is generally wanting. And it is surely seldom the case that a great original thinker puts his best work in his books. Schopenhauer compares thought to a lovely maiden. He who is visited by the one must hasten to commit it to paper, or it will vanish to return no more; just as he must make the other his own by a betrothal on pain of seeing her become a rival's bride. The world is governed by ideas; and many which might have changed the world's history have been thrown out in the careless intercourse of daily life, and, wanting a chronicler, have been clean forgotten. Johnson lives in the pages of his faithful Boswell when his *Rasselas* and his Dictionary itself are nought but names. It is equally untrue that we most resemble the objects of our veneration. The converse is the case: for men admire in others the very qualities which they are secretly conscious of not possessing themselves. The impulse which leads us to seek closer acquaintance with the lives of men of genius is a natural and a wholesome one. My lamented friend Dr Sambhu Chunder Mookerjee possessed the divine spark: and the story of his life, however imperfectly it may be told, is full of interest.

He came of the purest Brahman stock: having been thirty-fourth in descent from Sriharsa, one of the five "twice-born" whom Raja Adisur of Gaur summoned from Kanauj to give laws and religion to his subjects. This remote ancestor was himself a man of letters and is the reputed author of the last Indian Epic poem—*Naisadh Charita*, the history of King Nala who reigned in Nishadah, the modern Beder. That epoch-making doctrine, heredity, finds support in this instance of the transmission of intellectual power through five centuries. It must be admitted that the pursuit of Sambhu Chunder's immediate progenitors were hardly favourable to the conservation of literary energy.

Stern necessity had degraded them from the altar to the shop. His father Mothoor Mohun Mookerjee, far from posing as a visible manifestation of divinity, supported himself as a manufacturer and trader in the Calcutta Bazar. Nor on the other side were things more propitious. His mother was the daughter of Babu Raj Chandra Banarji, a Srotriya Brahman of Tara Atpur in Hugli, who sold firewood and oilseeds at Chitpore. Sambhu Chunder was born in May 1839 at his father's residence in Barnagore. He was an only son, and became the object of that idolatry which is lavished on such everywhere. The absence of early discipline will account for the waywardness which marred his highest endeavours in after life. At the age of five he was sent to a day-school kept in the house of a local zemindar. Here he was more remarkable for his pranks than for application to the rudiments of learning. The teacher, unable to correct his masterful pupil, reported him to his landlord, who is said to have punished the little rebel by putting him into a sack full of huge black ants. The child brooded over this insult and revenged it by privately inserting chillies and other noxious adulterants into the contents of the village tyrant's *hookah*. Play is the redundant energy given us for the support of the organism. Arnold of Rugby, the greatest of our modern pedagogues, said that he had great hopes for a really "naughty boy;" meaning that the intense vitality displayed in rebellious acts might be directed to useful ends. He would have been delighted with such a pupil as Sambhu Chunder. Mothoor Mohun Mookerjee was a Hindu of the fine old crusted type, who saw in the study of the *mlechcha's* tongue a potentiality for the seduction of his darling from the straight path of religious duty. But for a mere accident Sambhu Chunder might have lived and died a respectable merchant, and the Indian Press would have been far the poorer. One summer's day in 1848 he was led by curiosity to watch the pupils at the local missionary school playing a sort of rudimentary cricket. He was accosted by some of the seniors, and led to join the school. This defection aroused the paternal ire, but it had his mother's support : and, after a warm domestic debate, Sambhu Chunder was allowed to continue his studies at the sectarian seminary. But Mothoor Mohun's fears were soon excited by the conversion to Christianity of four Brahman pupils. Sambhu Chunder was hurried away from the dangerous medium and placed at the Oriental Seminary at Garanhatta in Calcutta. Here his natural quickness of intellect soon made itself felt. His father insisted on accompanying him to school daily, thence proceeding to his shop. But, as a Brahman of the straitest sect, he had various religious observances to get through before mundane affairs could claim his attention. Hence it was often high noon ere the lad entered the schoolroom. As a laggard he took his place at the tail of his class ; but he invariably closed the day's work at its head. Mothoor Mohun Mookerjee, unlike Charles Lamb, made amends for his tardy arrival on the scene of duty by staying there long after the ordinary business hours. The little Sambhu Chunder beguiled his long waitings at the residence of the Ghose family of Bagh Bazar. Some of its younger members were preparing for the Minor Scholarship Examination, and were wont to discuss knotty points amongst themselves in *Butler's Analogy*, *Paradise Lost*, and Shakespeare's plays. There is no more powerful stimulus to a plastic brain than the companionship of others more advanced who are of a studious turn. My subject's intellect was spurred to exertion by these debates. At first an awe-stricken listener, he soon became an active combatant. Nor was this all. To keep pace with his associates he needed close private study : and thus was formed that burning love for letters, that command of dialectics which distinguished him in after life. His father, who by this time had adopted his wife's views as to the nature of young hopeful's education, was induced to permit him to join the Calcutta Public Library. But the spectacle of a lad in his early teens reading with solemn elders had its ludicrous side. In order to escape the mild "chaff" lavished on him, he pored over his English classics while seated outside the Library in a pony-carriage his father had provided to take him to school and back. In 1853 the Hindoo Metropolitan College was opened by a knot of orthodox Hindus, as a sort of protest against the laxity displayed in the matter of religious teaching in the older institution. Its first Principal was Captain D. L. Richardson, who, with a full share of eccentricity, was one of the most cultured Englishmen who had made India their home. Sambhu Chunder entered the senior first class of the school, but soon migrated to the first year College class. Here he continued to be the centre of stimulating influences. His chosen associates were Kristodas Pal, destined like him to be a pillar of Indian Journalism, and Romesh Chunder and Sooresh Chunder of the Wellington Square Dutt family. Nor was he less fortunate in his teacher. Captain Richardson was struck with his acuteness and love of learning, and invited him to attend the private lectures on English literature which he was wont to give after school hours. His taste for composition was formed at the same time by the instruction of two other Professors of the college, Captain Harris and Mr. Kirkpatrick. The teacher of mathematics, Mr. William Masters, was attracted by the brilliant youth, and strove hard to instil into his mind the rudiments of his science. This, however, was an impossible task. Dr. Mookerjee retained till his dying day a profound dislike for this branch of study. He would have been a richer, and probably a better man had he wooed the coy goddess enthroned in figures.

While at the Hindoo Metropolitan College he

made his first plunge into the troubled sea of journalism. In association with his bosom friend Kristodas Pal he started a periodical called the *Calcutta Monthly Magazine.* Very precocious disquisitions on Sydney Smith, the Crimean War, and other topics of the day, appeared in its columns. The venture, however, was not long-lived, for the boy-editors had everything to learn as to the details of management: and the fitful appearance of the magazine soon exhausted the patience of their readers. Shortly afterwards he accepted the post of Editor of the *Morning Chronicle*, a daily paper owned by a Mr. Love. His politics were by no means in accord with those of his proprietor. The two found themselves at opposite poles with regard to Lord Dalhousie's policy in Oudh; and the young editor was compelled to vacate his chair. The disappointment might well have disgusted him with his chosen profession; but its attractions were irresistible. His leisure was devoted to inditing articles on burning questions in the *Hindu Intelligencer.*

At a time when old England was ringing with stories of military and naval disasters Dr. Johnson remarked that public woes deterred no man from eating his dinner as usual. People marry and are given in marriage while their country's destinies are trembling in the balance ; and Dr. Mookerjee gave hostages to fortune during the throes of the last great struggle for Empire, in 1857. His wife was a scion of the Bural family of Jorasnko. This event was far from having the sinister influence on his mental development which is assigned to early marriages by self-styled friends of India. They are stigmatized as the root of the decay which is consuming the country's manhood. That the children of the upper middle classes in many parts of Bengal are mere human weeds is but too evident : but the cause of deterioration must be sought for in adverse physical conditions rather than in a custom which is hallowed by the acquiescence of a hundred generations. Doctrinaire-reformers forget that human nature is more powerful than convention, and that the sexual instinct is far stronger and is manifested at an earlier stage of life in the tropics than in temperate regions. The institution of marriage regulates this overwhelming impulse, just as law does the equally powerful craving for revenge. Hence marriages in early life are good in themselves and a cause of good to society: and would-be reformers should ponder well the lessons afforded by countless ruined careers the outcome of an undue postponement of the nuptial rites.

Soon after his marriage, Mookerjee was introduced by his friend Sooresh Chunder Dutt to the late Hurish Chandra Mukerjee, Editor of the *Hindoo Patriot*, a man who, during his short life, exercised a greater influence over his country's development than any of his contemporaries. The journalist was deeply interested by the young man's conversation; and a life-long friendship was formed between them. It was probably Hurish Chandra's influence that led Mookerjee to turn his attention to the political outlook. Carried away by the general excitement he hastily put together a pamphlet exposing the secret history of the Sepoy revolt which was shaking the foundation of the empire. Lord Canning's "Gagging Act" had closed the Indian Press to political topics: and it became necessary to find a publisher at home. This was effected in 1857, through the agency of Mr. Malcolm Lewin, late Judge of the Madras Sudder Court, who had lost his appointment for having protested against alleged injustice done to Hindus in cases in which Christians were concerned. It made some sensation at home, and so close was the reasoning, so polished the diction that many believed it to be the work of an Englishman. His bosom friend Kristodas Pal had, by this time, entered active life as a translator in the District Judge's Office, Alipur; but Sambhu Chunder was in no haste to follow his example. He continued to pursue an even tenor of study, while seeking an honourable and independent employment. One soon presented itself in the shape of an Assistant-Secretaryship of the British Indian Association. As this office was virtually in the gift of his adviser Hurish Chandra Mukerjee, he had every reason to believe that it would be conferred on him. But in an unguarded moment he confided his ambition to a bosom friend, who made use of the information to secure the vacancy for himself. There are crises in the life of each of us when we must take counsel of ourselves alone and repress the generous impulse to confide in others. Dr. Mookerjee's disappointment at having been thus forestalled received some mitigation when the redoubtable editor of the *Hindoo Patriot* suggested that he should join the staff of the paper. He closed with the offer and became one of a little knot of brilliant youths who held the banner of Indian journalism higher than any of their successors have done.

He was not an ascetic of the elder Mill's type—one who preached and practised "low living and high thinking." Rather was he on the side of Benjamin Haydon, who cried "People may prate as much as they please of the pleasures of poverty: but I prefer champagne and the Order of the Bath!" His was essentially a convivial temperament ; and he was never so happy as when seated at a board spread with good things and surrounded by spirits congenial to his own. This tendency led him to dissipate his stores of nerve-power, and, indeed, laid the foundation of a malady to which he eventually succumbed. During the cold weather of 1858 he formed one of a party which met in the Barruipur Sub-division to celebrate a wedding in the family of Doctor Rajinder Dutt. A surfeit of oranges and green cocoanuts, followed by a severe chill, brought on an attack of asthma which undoubtedly curtailed his life. A native physician prescribed opium as a palliative : and

Sambhu Chunder joined the mighty army of consumers of the seductive drug. But he had more self-control than DeQuincey, and never became its slave. On the approach of a paroxysm of his malady he took a large dose of crude Turkey opium, but discontinued its use in the interval between the fits. Some one who knew his fellow creatures, I believe no less a personage than the Emperor Charles V., said that every man was either a fool or a physician at forty. Long before reaching that crucial age, Dr. Mookerjee became an example of the truth of this apothegm. In association with Rajinder and Romesh Chunder Dutt he threw himself with ardour into the study of the then (1861) novel science of Homœopathy. Dr. Berigny, one of its leading European exponents, was invited by them to put its theories in practice in Calcutta. A dispensary was organized for him in Lal Bazar, where it still stands and bears his name. Sambhu Chunder was one of his closest allies. His study became a laboratory, and he communicated the results of his experiment with no little pride to the leading homœopaths of Chicago and Philadelphia. In recognition of his researches he received the degree of M.D. from an American University. Such was the origin of the learned title of which Mookerjee was pardonably proud. He never sought a degree from his own *Alma Mater* ; and it is not to the credit of that body that one of her greatest sons should never have been vouchsafed an honorary one. But, as we shall presently see, he was not a self-seeker : and we have it on high authority that a prophet has no honour in his own country.

To most men, wrote Sir Henry Taylor, author of *Philip Van Artevelde*, habits of obedience come more naturally than habits of command. It is this pliability in human nature which alone makes civilization possible. Some there are who, without the power of impressing their will on others, are incapable of discipline, and such men are grits in the wheels of human progress. Obedience is, therefore, the first lesson which a child should learn. It must not be carried too far, lest the unique personality which each of us possesses should be warped or crushed ; and the difficulty of striking a happy mean in this respect renders education the tremendous task it is. Mookerjee's training was very far from being an ideal one. His intellect was forced at the expense of his moral sense ; and to end of his life he retained many characteristics of a spoiled child. Impatient of control, wayward and impulsive, he brought into play but a small portion of his great talents and dissipated energies which, if properly used, would have made him a leader of men. We find him "everything by turns and nothing long :" and it was only when life's shadows began to lengthen that he settled down in the literary path, looking neither to the right hand nor to the left.

After two years' work on the *Hindoo Patriot* he suddenly resolved to be a "limb of the law," and became an articled clerk in the office of

Messrs. Allan, Judge and Lingham. But he was not long in finding out that the profession was one wholly unsuited to his genius; and the death of his mother, to whom he was devotedly attached, occurring on the eve of the Attorney's Examination, he bade farewell for the time to law books. He was welcomed back by his friend Hurish Chunder Mookerjee and formally appointed Sub-Editor of the *Hindoo Patriot*. During the next three years he virtually edited that paper: for his chief was seized by a sickness to which, after a prolonged struggle, he succumbed. Mookerjee became his biographer: and his work bears eloquent testimony to his own culture, as well as to the merit of his benefactor. Though poor Hurish Chunder was cut off at 39, he left a profound and abiding impression behind him. Like his annalist he came of a Kulin stock; but, unlike him, he was thrown penniless on the world at the outset of active life, and his education was laboriously acquired in the scanty leisure left by absorbing duties. While still a boy he became a clerk in a Calcutta mercantile house; and, years afterwards, was promoted to similar but better paid functions in a Government office, which he held till his death. The story of the *Hindoo Patriot's* birth and vigorous youth is told in this biography. The paper arose from the ashes of the *Bengal Recorder*, one of the ephemerides which herald the awakening of a nation's literary spirit. The proprietor found it a losing speculation: and in June 1854 offered the press and good will for a mere song. Hurish Chunder who had been one of the leading contributors, saw an opportunity of gratifying a darling ambition, and became the purchaser. The transaction was veiled in secrecy, for his master, the Military Auditor General, would hardly have approved of a proprietor-editor of a journal as one of his subordinates. The "man of straw" put forward was an elder brother, Babu Haran Chandra Mukherji; but the entire labour of editing and management fell on Hurish. The struggle was long and severe: and at one time the poor *kerani's* salary was taxed to the extent of Rs. 100 a month to meet the deficit in income. He bore the ordeal with heroic courage, which was at last rewarded by the pecuniary success of his venture. His untimely death, however, robbed his family of the benefit they might have derived from a fine literary property. Babu Kaliprasanna Singha, the Bengali translator of the *Mahabharata*, purchased the paper from the executors, and satisfied the claim of the *benamdar* by a trifling solatium.

In the course of 1860, Dr. Mookerjee wrote a pamphlet containing a powerful indictment of the policy of Mr. James Wilson who had been sent out to restore equilibrium to the shattered finances of the Empire. One of his expedients for refilling the exchequer was the cordially-hated Income Tax, which violates nearly all the essentials laid down by economists as those of an equitable assessment. Nor is its author alone attacked. The then Viceroy,

Lord Canning, comes in for a share of invective which would be impossible in these decorous days. The history of his selection as Viceroy is told, I believe, for the first time, thus :—" The Prime Minister of England exercises an almost divine prerogative in influencing by a single choice the fortunes of two hundred millions of his fellow creatures. People, however, come to entertain very low ideas of the ministerial sense of responsibility when they learn what considerations lead to the choice of Governor-General. One is a cousin to be provided for; another is better abroad; and as for Tom, he was a fine fellow at College. It is reported that when Lord Palmerston was asked the sort of 'mute inglorious Miltonism' which his penetrating vision discerned in Lord Canning to entitle him to his present appointment, he naively exclaimed,—'Ah, well, well, his father was the first man who gave me a place in the Cabinet and—.'" The pamphleteer's views have much of the crudeness of youth about them. He lays down the truism that Government is but a question of rupees, annas and pice, and that it must be judged by the practical success of its financial measures. But he goes on to argue that the obnoxious impost is opposed to the spirit of the Queen's Proclamation ; that taxation of all kinds implies popular representation. He did not reflect that the times were not propitious for experiments in the art of ruling. The India of 1858 had but just emerged from a civil war which had drenched her fairest provinces with blood : and her maladies needed firm as well as sympathetic treatment. De Tocqueville sounds a note of wholesome warning when he remarks that there is no period so fraught with danger to a bad Government as that in which it enters on a course of attempted reform. The events of 1857 showed that ours then came within the category.

The new proprietor of the *Hindoo Patriot* was a youthful millionarie with generous—too generous—instincts. Dr. Mookerjee vainly strove to avert the ruin foreshadowed by his employer's extravagance: and when he found that his own reputation would be sullied by further association with a spendthrift, he sought another sphere of work. He finally closed with an offer made him by Babu Dakhina Ranjan Mookerjee, who, after a chequered career, had established himself as a landowner in Oudh, to proceed to Lucknow as Secretary of the brand-new Taluqdars' Association. Under the auspices of that body he edited a weekly journal in English called *Samachar Hindustani*, in opposition to a local Anglo-Indian journal edited by a bitter opponent of the Taluqdars. Mookerjee soon showed that he carried too many guns for his antagonist. The latter's paper collapsed and he beat a retreat; while Mookerjee was hailed as a deliverer by the Taluqdars trembling for their new status. It was while editing the *Samachar Hindustani* that Mookerjee had frequent passages at arms with Dr. D. B. Smith who was then in charge of a little paper called *The Hills* issued from Mussooree. In these encounters Mookerjee proved his resourcefulness and ability for controversy. From Lucknow he also sent contributions to the *Hindoo Patriot* which was under the charge of his friend Rai Kristodas Pal Bahadur. During his stay there he took lessons from that sweet singer Miah Amir Ali, grandson of the famous Shori Miah, the Verdi of Hindustani music. Throughout his life he cherished a passionate love for that beautiful art, which satisfied the cravings of his emotional nature. Gœthe has laid down as the three essentials of culture that a man must never spend a day without listening to good music, gazing on a splendid picture, or conversing with a lovely woman. The first, and perhaps the last, are difficult but not impossible of attainment in India; but the second, appreciation of which evidences a far higher degree of refinement, is utterly beyond the reach of Indian youth. A Government which disposed of scores of millions hardly possesses a single picture worthy of study. Mookerjee's enjoyment of music was intense. It is related of him that a few years before his death he was a guest at one of those splendid entertainments given by the great Houses of Calcutta to celebrate the Durga Puja. Ravished by the melody produced by the best artists of our day, he was called back to a sordid world by the ill-timed chattering of a man who, a millionaire like the host, began prating of the subject nearest and dearest to him—money. The Doctor withered his interlocutor with a glance and stalked out of the hall in disgust.

We have seen how Mookerjee's caprice and distaste for routine led him into the cardinal error of changing his profession. The same defects militated against his success as an employé. It is, indeed, difficult to conceive a nature less pliable than his, less prone to subject his own will to the whim of a master.

Service, the old proverb hath it, is no inheritance: but it has the immense advantage of disciplining the mind and teaching a lesson which Mookerjee was fated never to learn—self-control. In 1864 he was introduced by his close friend the Nawab Abdool Luteef Bahadoor to the Nawab Nazim of Bengal who still kept up a semblance of majesty* on very inadequate resources at Murshidabad. The Nazim had fallen out with his Dewan, and was seeking to replace him. Mookerjee's evident culture and his distinguished manners caught

* I became intimate with this unfortunate Prince while I was officiating as Magistrate of Murshidabad in 1883. He was always preceded in his walks abroad by a Chobdar who proclaimed his style and titles in a loud voice, a ceremony, by the way, which was adopted by an Anglo-Indian of high official rank as lately as 1825. The Nazim Mansur Ali was a loveable and accomplished man: and more than one of his sons would have gained distinction but for their birth in a threadbare purple. Those who knew and still lament poor Sultan Saheb will agree with me.

his fancy ; and he appointed him Political Adviser and soon afterwards Dewan. Here Mookerjee found himself in the vortex of a whirlpool of intrigue. The discarded minister had a strong following among the *amla ;* and every action of his successor was misrepresented. He failed, too, in the caution necessary in so ticklish an office. Drastic changes were carried into effect which raised a nest of hornets about his ears. Amongst them was a reduction in the perquisites of the eunuchs—a class which wields immense, if occult, influence in an Oriental Court. Echoes of the intense irritation that resulted reached Mookerjee's father, then grievously ill at Baranagore, who sent a nephew with strict injunctions to bring his too daring son home at any cost. The young Dewan, however, stuck to his guns, for a retreat would have given his foes cause to rejoice. More active measures on their part followed. Mookerjee's house was beset by a gang of ruffians : and but for the timely arrival of the Police, he would have suffered the gravest indignities. Then the law was prostituted to serve private spite. A false information was given to the District Magistrate, the late Mr. W. L. Heeley, to the effect that the Dewan had misappropriated state papers: and the Joint-Magistrate of Murshidabad city was induced to attempt a search of his house. The official was met on the threshold by Mookerjee, who begged a hearing ere unmerited disgrace should be inflicted on him. A parley ensued: and the Magistrate was inclined to believe that the story told him was false. The band of accusers, however, were urgent in repeating their calumnies. He was hesitating when an express came from Mr. Heeley directing an immediate suspension of proceedings. His enemies were baffled; but the too ardent reformer was not destined to trouble them much longer. He was summoned to Calcutta to perform his father's funeral rites and returned no more to the scene of his first essay in administration. A suit was afterwards brought against him by the Naib Dewan, claiming damages for the alleged loss of documents confided to his care. A move which might have been his ruin redounded to his advantage. Not only did he succeed in proving to the court the groundlessness of the charge, but he established a counter-claim for a large sum due as pay and commission for purchases made in Calcutta, which was recovered from the plaintiff.

Mookerjee's day-dreams of glory to be acquired in the sphere of politics ended, he was fain to return to the *Hindoo Patriot.* Among reviews written by him at this period were those on Sir William Hunter's *Annals of Rural Bengal*, a work which at once placed its young author in the foremost rank of men of letters. His discrimination and wide reading eminently fitted him to shine as a reviewer: and he had the rarest of qualities—that of withholding praise where none was due. But his love of change was incessantly spurring him to seek new fields of labour. He was offered the headmastership of the Calcutta Training Academy:

and after some hesitation accepted it. The "twice-boiled cabbage," as Juvenal calls it, of the school-room was even less to his taste than the drudgery of office: and his career as a dominie was a brief one. It was not without a beneficial influence on his development; for while residing at the Hindu Hostel as Principal he became the centre of a coterie which included the fine flower of the Indian intellect of the day. Amongst them were Babus Krishna Kamal Bhattacharjya, now Principal of the Ripon College; Syama Charan Ganguli, who fills similar functions in the Uttarpara institution; Dwarka Nath Mitter, the most learned and unspoiled of Indian Judges; Syama Charan Dey, greatest of Indian Accountants; and the late Ashutosh Mookerjee, the first Premchand-Raychand Scholar. These and other lesser lights of that generation met regularly at Mookerjee's quarters and beguiled the hours of night by discussing Fichte, Comte and Schopenhauer.

But the charms of these symposia were far from making amends for the irksomeness of a difficult and thankless profession. In 1868 he fell in readily with advice given by his friend Nawab Abdool Luteef Bahadoor to accept an offer of the post of Secretary made by the Raja Sheoraj Singh of Kashipur. His new employer had recently obtained a seat on the Viceregal Legislative Council: and, being a noble of the old school, found his ignorance of English a serious obstacle in that august assembly. Mookerjee was engaged to be his "ghost," in modern literary slang, and accompanied him to Kashipur. The Raja's servants had celebrated their master's approaching return by a great hunting expedition, in the course of which they laid a mighty boar low. The first sight that met the former's eyes on entering his palace was the dead monster laid out for his inspection, surrounded by a group of exultant *shikaris*. Overjoyed at the happy omen, he ordered the noble quarry to be divided, and sent a goodly portion of the meat to his new Secretary. Mookerjee found himself in a dilemma. As became a staunch Brahman, he was a vegetarian : while a strict adherence to his tenets would cause offence to his patron. The dread of losing caste prevailed ; and he sent back the obnoxious haunch. The Raja strove hard to conquer Mookerjee's scruples : and even assembled Pandits to decide the knotty point. Their verdict was to the effect that wild boar's flesh was not tabooed by the Shastras. But Mookerjee, though "convinced against his will," still respectfully declined the present. It is to the Raja's credit that he showed no resentment at this display of independence ; and warmly recommended his sturdy follower to the notice of the Nawab of Rampur who needed a Personal Assistant. Mookerjee was invited to Rampur and soon gained great influence over the chief—so great, indeed, that the jealousy of the leading courtiers was evoked. Unable to tolerate a Hindu in a position of trust about their sovereign, they intrigued hard to prevent his final and formal appointment to the vacant post. The outcome was delay and excuses ; and when the Nawab made a definite offer to Mookerjee, it was clogged with the condition that he should give up all relations with a brother of whom the chief was intensely jealous. Now a friendship, dating from his stay in Murshidabad, united Mookerjee to this scion of the Rampur House. He nobly refused to sacrifice it to a prospect of wordly advantage, and left the Rampur territories. While making arrangements for a tour in the Upper Provinces which would have embraced Jaipur and probably changed the current of his life, he was recalled to Calcutta by the news of his wife's serious illness. As I have already related, the issue was long and doubtful : but skilful medical help and her husband's unceasing devotion at length restored her to her family. In the intervals of watching at the invalid's beside he found time to edit a

Magazine * which bore his name and had a very fair circulation until merged in the larger venture of *Reis and Rayyet.* Nor was the *Hindoo Patriot,* the arena of his early journalistic efforts, forgotten. In its columns appeared a biography of that curious phenomenon, the Begum Sekandra of Bhopal, which has profound in-

* The first series extended from February to June 1861, altogether five numbers. The second ran from July 1872 to December 1876, ten numbers being issued every year. The celebrated "Baroda Yellow Book" belonged to this series. It was a scathing attack on the abortive attempt to judge the unfortunate ruler Mulhar Rao by a council of his peers. When it came out, it created a great sensation. Lord Northbrook admired it highly although it was an unsparing criticism of his proceedings towards Mulhar Rao. For a long time it was believed to be the production of Mr. Montriou, then a prominent member of the Calcutta bar. The ability displayed appeared so great that those who did not know Mookerjee well could not believe that a native could write so vigorously and show so complete a mastery of the details of criminal law, of Indian politics and of the intrigues of native courts.

terest for those who advocate the fullest play for woman's faculties. The most conservative must admit that when an Indian female has been vested with power, she has generally used it to greater advantage than the majority of rulers belonging to the stronger sex as it is called.

The law always exercised a strange fascination on Mookerjee. We have already seen that he was unable to endure the long probation required by the attorney's profession. As the attainment of the status of Pleader made no such demands on his patience, he appeared at the annual examination at Allahabad, but a severe attack of asthma cut short his efforts as a candidate. He was soon recalled to Calcutta to preside at his daughter's marriage ; and did not return to the capital of the North-Western Provinces. During the next year or two he was absorbed in press work ; but the nomad spirit finally became too strong for resistance. In the winter of 1876 he waited on His Highness the Maharaja of Jaipur,* who was on a visit to Calcutta, and a friendship began which is creditable to the memory of both. Soon afterwards he noticed an advertisement in the *Indian Daily News* announcing the

* Maharaja Ram Sing of Jaipur was a sincere admirer of talent. He had heard of Mookerjee many years previously. As one of the Commissioners selected by Lord Northbrook for trying Mulhar Rao on the accusation of Colonel Phayre, the Maharaja had personal interest in the Baroda number of *Mookerjee's Magazine.* He had heard that the book was a very able impeachment of Lord Northbrook's Baroda policy and that many new arguments were addressed to the reader bringing out the innocence of Mulhar Rao. The whole question, again, of the relations of the native chiefs to the Paramount Power was discussed for the first time by an Indian scholar of reputation who was thoroughly conversant with everything published on that topic. Maharaja Ram Sing, it is said, caused the book to be translated into Urdu and read to him. Having mastered its contents in this way, he formed a very high idea of the abilities of Mookerjee. The very next time he came to Calcutta, he sent

Maharaja of Hill Tippera's desire to appoint a successor to his minister Babu Nilmoni Das. He immediately submitted an application, of which he heard nothing for many months. Then came an autograph letter

---

his trusted adviser Babu Kanti Chandra Mookerjee to see our Doctor and arrange an interview. Babu Kanti Chandra had at one time been a teacher in the Janai school and was well known to Mookerjee's friend, the lamented Babu Jadu Nath Ghose of the Seals' Free College of Calcutta, "the Arnold of India," as Kristodas Pal used to call him. With Babu Jadu Nath, Kanti Chandra came to Dr. Mookerjee and arranged the much-desired interview. The Doctor was received with great cordiality by Maharaja Ram Sing. His polished conversation, his thorough command of Urdu, and the range of his information, at once struck his illustrious host, who was no mean judge of human nature. The impression made by him on the Maharaja created deep jealousy among certain officials of Jaipur. When he next went to visit the Maharaja he was kept waiting for a long time in the hope that he would feel annoyed and go away. But the old official of the Nizamat knew enough of the ways of native

from the Maharaja which announced its receipt but enquired the reason of the inordinate delay in forwarding it. Mookerjee saw that his letter had been detained owing to palace intrigues: and, acting under His Highness's

courts to attach much importance to these tactics. He waited and at last the *Ittala* (information) had to be sent. When the Maharaja met him, the usual polite enquiries were exchanged. Dr. Mookerjee informed his host of what had happened. The Maharaja called his superior officials and attendants, and warned them seriously, saying that Dr. Mookerjee had not come of his own accord, but that he was an invited and honoured guest. If, after the warning, anybody dared to delay in sending the *Ittala*, the Maharaja knew how to behave towards him. With many apologies for the rudeness of his servants, the Maharaja dismissed Mookerjee earlier than he had wished. The latter, before his departure, took care to impress upon one official in particular that his jealousy was causeless, for he had not the remotest wish to supplant him, or, indeed, to enter the Maharaja's service. The Prince soon afterwards died to the great regret of all who admired statesmanlike qualities in a ruler.—Note by Babu Kisari Mohan Ganguli.

advice, he sent a second application which was immediately complied with. He was appointed Minister of Hill Tippera on a salary of Rs. 500 per mensem with a residence and various other perquisites probably amounting to as much more in value. In December 1877 he proceeded to his new sphere of action. It was one even less suited to a man of his tastes than Murshidabad had been. There he had been within easy reach of the capital, at a court still retaining some of the amenities which had distinguished it while its master ruled Bengal, Behar and Orissa. Tippera was a congeries of low hills clad with trackless jungle, then on the easternmost confines of British territory. The Maharaja was a man of culture and even erudition: but his sons were still boys and the rest of his family plunged in pristine barbarism. Society, so far as it existed at all at the capital, Agartala, was in the same plight. Mookerjee was cut off from the cheerful ways of man as completely as Ovid, that sweetest singer of the

Augustan age, when banished by imperial jealousy to the shores of the Black Sea. Nor was his outlook, from an official point of view, more promising. The little state was torn by dissensions arising from the "Great Water Question," as it was called. Like the rulers of most of our hill territories, the Maharaja was fully persuaded that he was of pure Kshatriya stock, a descendant of the Lunar race: but many good Hindus believed as firmly that alliances in the past with non-Aryan mountaineers have suilled the purity of his descent. Such sceptics declined to take water from his hands, though no Brahman would scruple to accept a draught from a genuine member of the warriour caste. Others were less scrupulous: and in process of time this shibboleth was extracted from all candidates from office. The Maharaja never reflected that a man capable of sacrificing his religious prejudices to wordly profit* was not likely to be a trusty servant or

* The institution of monarchy has its advantages:

a disinterested adviser. Hence, bad counsels prevailed : the palace became a hot-bed of intrigues : and greater importance was attached to hoodwinking the European political Agent than executing indispensable reforms. Mookerjee found his endeavours for the public good constantly thwarted by unseen influences. An estrangement from his master followed, due in part to the latter's weakness, but also, it must be admitted, to Mookerjee's pride and that excessive sensitiveness which anticipates a slight. Things came to a climax in October 1879 ; when he learnt that a sanhedrim of Pandits from

but honourable men must doubt whether they are not counterbalanced by the debauchery of public morals caused by certain of its phases. It appears to be admitted that any man has a right to barter his religion for a throne. Henry IV. of France did so, and his pithy excuse "Paris is well worth a mass" is quoted in his extenuation by good Protestants. His example has been repeatedly followed, notably by the father of the king of the Belgians, and by the present Czarina of all the Russias.

Eastern Bengal was being secretly planned in view of obtaining an authoritative recognition of the Maharaja's claims. Not only was he offended at the evident want of confidence in himself thus displayed, but he foresaw failure and disgrace involving all who were, or were presumed to be, advisers of the Maharaja. He, therefore, resolved to abandon a false position; and proceeded to Calcutta with a determination to return no more to the Hill Territory. To pursue this Tippera episode to its close: the Maharaja retained a profound sense of his minister's intellectual powers and made more than one attempt to win him back. While on his way to Brindaban in 1884, he induced Mookerjee to accept the post of paid Adviser, on the understanding that Calcutta, and not Agartala, should be his head-quarters. It is characteristic of my subject's utter disregard for pelf that he took no effectual steps to obtain the salary attached to his office, though it was regularly provided for in the state budget, thus surrendering nearly Rs. 20,000 in the aggregate. In 1885 I became Magistrate of the British district of Tippera and *ex officio* Political Agent of the Hill Territory. Like most of my colleagues who have held that office I strove hard to restore equilibrium to the finances and to raise the character of the administration. My efforts were misrepresented by the "reptile press;" and to my surprise I found *Reis and Rayyet*—of which more anon—ranged on the side of brass-bound conservatism. Now, I am impervious to anonymous press attacks.* "As the world educates men to become indifferent to praise

* Those who take delight in setting Europeans and natives by the ears are the worst enemies of their country. If any impression is to be made on the dense phalanxes of ignorance and superstition around us, men of enlightenment of both communities must stand shoulder to shoulder. It is impossible to exaggerate the mischief done to India by the want of charity and good feeling, the habitual misrepresentations indulged in by a certain section of the native press

and censure, as neither perfection nor devotion ensures its favour, misfortunes ensure its contempt, success its envy and hate, the best course is to seek the approval of one's own conscience." But the case was different when I saw a man whom I respected misled by persons interested in the maintenance of gross abuses. I, therefore, gave Mookerjee a candid account of the facts on which my action had been based. He replied in a conciliatory strain, and animadversions in his paper ceased. I deeply regret not having preserved the correspondence which passed between us. Mookerjee's private letters, like his literary work, have a distinct flavour of their own,—and I never knew a more complete illustration of the saying "a man's style is himself."

On Mookerjee's return to civilization he was named by the Chief Justice of Bengal a member of a Commission appointed for the partition of the estates of the Rani Rashmani. He entered on these functions with zest: for he had known the deceased lady ; and had qualified her as "a remarkable woman who, as one of the greatest land-owners in this country, a she-Crœsus of Calcutta, had managed to foil the eagles of the period." Alas! her property, governed with consummate care during her life-time, became the prey of less noble birds after her death. Amongst them—in a figurative sense, of course—I must include the legal tribe and the commissioners for the partition. This is always a tedious process, and it is not shortened by the system of remuneration adopted by the High Court—a fee of five gold mohurs to each commissioner for a sitting.

In 1882 he founded the well known weekly paper *Reis and Rayyet* which has always been conspicuous for literary finish and generally for breadth of view. Here at length he found his proper place—an editorial chair from which he could deal with the topics of the day in his own peculiar vein—the professor's, tempered with a certain dry humour. No weekly periodical, not even the *Hindoo Patriot* in the days of Kristodas Pal, enjoyed a degree of influence approaching that of *Reis and Rayyet.* It brought Mookerjee into confidential relations with the makers of history. Lord Dufferin, amongst others, was his constant correspondent. It sobered his judgment, and deepened his sense of responsibility. Finally, it anchored him to a position for which he was especially fitted.

The intervals between his editorial labours in 1883 were occupied in the production of his *Travels in E. Bengal*—a rich and fertile tract to which he was bound by ties of ancestral sympathy. The book is rather prolix and desultory: but it contains some wonderful pieces of word-painting. The reader is penetrated by the subtle influences of nature as manifested in those Netherlands of Bengal. The skies lit up by sunsets of transcendant beauty or darkened by masses of rolling cloud; the broad expanses of vivid green broken only by the clumps of graceful foliage which mark the jealously-guarded penates of a wealthy peasantry; the majestic rivers covered with outlandish crafts whose pattern has not altered since Vikramaditya reigned and Manu laid down the law; the swirl of the tall rice plants against one's boat as it is vigorously impelled by the black but comely gondoliers;—all come back to him who, possessing local knowledge, peruses this record of travel. Not less will he acknowledge the unfeigned goodness of heart which underlies an affected cynicism. In May 1884 he came prominently before the public in a new capacity—that of after-dinner speaker. There are few faculties rarer than that which enables a man to make a creditable display in that character: and he showed that he possessed it in a marked degree. I was present on the occasion—a public dinner given at the Raja of Paikpara's Calcutta mansion in honour of Mr. Joubert, the organizer of the International Exhibition of 1883, and was introduced to Dr. Mookerjee by my old friend Mr. W. H. Grimley, now Commissioner of Chota-Nagpur. Dr. Johnson said of Burke that no one could spend five minutes in his company while sheltering himself from a shower under an archway without discovering that he was an extraordinary man. My experience of Mookerjee reminded me of this remark. We were neighbours at table and I had ample opportunity of observing him. He looked much older than his years and his spare frame and deeply-lined features gave one the idea of a man long past his prime. His face was of the highest Aryan type, his eyes penetrating and luminous, while sedate humour played round his mobile lips. We soon became absorbed in colloquy to the neglect, I fear, of the banquet and the other guests around us. The Doctor's originality of mind was not less conspicuous than his memory. The first enabled him to pour forth the quaintest criticisms of men and things: the second to illustrate his views by a flood of apt quotations. These pre-occupations did not prevent his acquitting himself more than creditably as an orator. He instituted a masterly comparison between the great Show on the eve of closing and its predecessors since 1851. Shortcomings were not concealed, but due credit was given for the dauntless energy which triumphed over so many obstacles. "India," he said, "had neither the soil nor the elasticity enjoyed by young and vigorous communities; but presented the arid rocks and deserts of an effete civilization, hardly stirred to a semblance of life by a foreign occupation dozing over its easily-gained advantages." He was cheered to the echo; and there were some present who regretted that gifts so rare had not found wider scope in his country's service.

We are told that a nation's vitality may be measured by the length of the interval between the attainment of full growth in the average unit and the advent of old age. The longer this period of lusty prime, the more intense is the vitality of the race: and when decay sets in as soon as complete development is reached, the extinction of the race is within measurable distance. Few, indeed, of the inhabitants of the Gangetic delta reach the span of seventy years, allotted by King David as the extreme limit of human life, but which now, thanks to physical education and the spread of sanitary knowledge, is regarded as indicating the confines merely of old age. Mookerjee, when our acquaintance began, was only 46 and looked 60. Three years later, in 1886, he showed unmistakable signs of breaking up. The attacks of his old foe, the asthma, became acuter and more frequent: and opium ceased to give him complete relief. The time was one of fierce journalistic activity: for the third and last Burmese war was in progress and its events demanded close vigilance. His attitude as regards the then Viceroy's policy was eminently characteristic of his bent of mind. He held in abhorrence anything savouring of greed and injustice and regarded the invasion of King Theebaw's territories, inevitable as we now know it to have been, with deep suspicion. But when he found that the "reptile press" made the campaign a peg on which to hang disloyal attacks on the British Government, he rallied to the side of order, and was the first among native journalists to declare his frank acceptance of established facts. The sedentary habits engendered by early neglect and confirmed by the exigencies of his profession impaired the elasticity of his constitution. In 1890 he was warned by a terrible attack of pneumonia that the sands of his life were running out. It is to the credit of his townsfolk of Baranagore that his seeming recovery should have evoked a public thanksgiving there. Thenceforward he was too evidently a broken man. Acute chest troubles followed the slightest chill or indiscretion in diet: and each attack left him permanently weaker. It is to this cause that his death was directly due. On the 26th January, 1894, he complained, on awaking, of difficulty of breathing : and was alarmed by the absence of the cough and expectoration which had always given him relief. On the 2nd February fever supervened ; and his life-long friend, Dr. Mahendra Lal Sircar, at once detected symptoms of pneumonia. Throughout the phases of this most distressing malady his mind continued clear and his judgment calm : and he was able to dictate bulletins to his medical adviser, detailing each step of his progress towards the end. On the 6th February he sank into a state of nervous prostration, worn out by insomnia and struggling with his cruel foe. On Wednesday the 7th he woke apparently much better ; but, alas, it was one of those fleeting Indian summers which deceive those gathered round a bed of death ! At three P. M., the final stage set in. It was prolonged for nearly four hours : and then the laboured breathing stopped and the large heart was still for ever.

It is difficult for a European, however deep his sympathies may be for all his fellow-creatures born like him to sorrow, to comprehend the inner working of a nature so complex as Sambhu Chunder Mookerjee's. The ground-work was, of course, his Hindu origin. He was not for nought the descendant of thirty generations of high priests: and he consistently stood by his order. For the greater part of his life he rigidly abstained from animal food and even fish. In the closing years increasing weakness rendered a stimulating diet indispensable; but it was adopted with the greatest reluctance, and in deference to his friends' entreaties. His inherited prejudices were continually at war with those liberal impulses which were the growth of a life-long devotion to letters. Thus he was always ready to welcome those of his countrymen who had outraged unenlightened public opinion by crossing the seas; and he once advised a friend, who consulted him as to the readiest method of gaining notoriety, to visit Europe and take his wife with him. But after receiving a visit from one of the "England returned" he always ordered the *hookahs* used during the call to be emptied and cleaned, and everything polluted by his touch to be destroyed. In this struggle between inbred conviction and acquired culture, the latter was, on the whole, victorious. His entire life was a protest against that foolish and, indeed, suicidal doctrine which lays down that there is no excellence of life or thought beyond the Hindu pale. Mahomedans were to be found amongst his closest friends : and he would frequently expatiate on the contrast between the exquisite courtesy of high-born followers of the Prophet and the thinly-disguised barbarism of so many "educated" Hindus. The late Nawab Abdool Luteef Bahadur, who in good breeding could have given points to Lord Chesterfield, was one of his inseparables. On one occasion they stood together as leaders of a distinctly Mahomedan movement. During the last Russo-Turkish war, the Nawab organized a public meeting for the purpose of congratulating the Turks on their early successes at Plevna. Sir Richard Temple, then Lieutenant-Governor, regarded the demonstration as one likely to offend Muscovite susceptibilities, and forbade it. Mookerjee was appealed to by the aggrieved Mahomedans : and he advised an appeal being made to higher influences. This was done : the inhibition was removed and the meeting duly held. He promptly sent a copy of the proceedings to the Premier, Lord Beaconsfield, and received a letter conveying his acknowledgments. The same breadth of mental vision led him to distrust the so-called " national " movement which aims at teaching men to swim without going into the water. He regarded the Congress and all its works as premature and as inspired by ignorance of mankind. Still colder was his sympathy for that foolish and dangerous agitation ostensibly directed at the conservation of the cow. His attitude here was not due to any disregard for the interests of the brute creation, but to an acquaintance with the secret springs which move the wire-pullers. He was a firm friend to English rule because his instincts told him that it was not only the best but the only possible rule; and because it was transparently inspired by a deep sense of justice. Justice, indeed, was far more really his god than any of the divinities of his Pantheon. His gorge rose at a tale of wrong: and thus his impulsive nature often led him to pour forth unmeasured diatribes on men and measures which calm reflection showed him to be in no way deserving of censure. His acquiescence in the politically inevitable did not militate against a becoming racial pride. Mookerjee unconsciously plagiarized King George the Third's utterance on a memorable occasion, and gloried in the name of Bengali.* He always fired up when his countrymen were traduced, as they often are, by critics who are

* His Majesty publicly declared at the outset of his reign that he "gloried in the name of Briton."

content to take their opinions secondhand.*

With aristocratic tastes and a love of sumptuous surroundings—Mookerjee's library was one of the best in India—his heart went out to fellow-creatures less fortunately placed. He felt as keenly as Cicero did the brotherhood of man. It is told of him that while waiting one day in his carriage at the door of a Chowringhee mansion, he was accosted by a degraded specimen of the genus "loafer," with the usual whining plea for charity. After complying, he entered into an earnest conversation with the "mean white," and learnt, as he told a friend,

* Sir F. Mouat, once Inspector-General of Jails, whose experience had been mostly of the residuum, told the London Statistical Society in 1867 that he "was one of those who considered that, in the matter of truth and honesty, the Bengalis were neither better nor worse than many nations boasting of a higher civilization and a purer faith; and that they in no degree merited the wholesale condemnation with which they were generally visited by those who wrote and talked much but really knew very little of them."

much curious information as to the ways of the class of which he would otherwise have been ignorant.* In his morning walks he used often to stop and chat with the Municipal sweepers,

* I was once told a story of failure in a similar quest by a great painter. He was commanded to dine and sleep at Windsor Castle, and entered the royal abode valet-less and carrying his own carpet bag. Shown into his bedroom, he knelt down to unpack his belongings, leaving the door open. While thus engaged, he was accosted by a flunkey, gorgeous in red and gold, who "supposed he was that painter-chap's man," and invited to "come down to the servants' hall, where he would be put up to the ways of the place." He gladly assented, when who should pass but his friend the Marchioness of Ely ! "Why, my dear Sir E—," she said, "I had no idea we were to have you so soon !" While conversing with her ladyship he glanced at poor "Jeames," and could not avoid laughing at his open-mouthed distress. After she had sailed on, he received next the abject apologies, which he accepted with great *bonhomie*, and reminded his interlocutor of his promise to "put him up to the ways of the place." "Oh no, Sir," was the reply, "I could not think of doing so."

questioning them as to their caste and social customs. On one occasion he engaged in a discussion with a palki-bearer whose acuteness had often attracted his attention. So high rose the tide of argument that the time slipped by and the cook's summons to supper was disregarded. A friend who had been invited to spend the evening with him was in high dudgeon at the delay, and received his excuses with bad grace. His servants were treated as humble friends; and their comfort deemed of higher importance than his own. Thus he never had a lamp burning in his room at night, for trimming and replenishing with oil would have needed constant attention. When a servant had retired to rest he was never disturbed on any pretext. Mookerjee would, on such occasions, attend to the *hookahs* himself and bring anything needed for the comfort of guests with his own hands. His regard for the interests of friends knew no bounds. His time, brains and money were equally at their call. So difficult did he find it to say "no," that he often escaped importunity by concealing himself. This prodigality in well-doing seriously crippled his resources, and prevented his making anything like the provision for his family which is every day effected by men without a tithe of his mental gifts, but also without a tithe of his milk of human kindness. Towards the close of his life Mookerjee was often tormented by doubts as to whether he had not shown an excessive degree of altruism. On one occasion, when hard-pressed by the necessity of providing for a daughter's marriage expenses, he bethought him of a friend, who had long owed him a considerable sum ; and while hinting at the necessity of repayment, he remarked that he had at last found out that a man's best ally was the "almighty dollar." It was a high-minded contempt for sordid questions of profit that gave him that sturdy independence, perhaps, his noblest trait. He was as incorruptible as Andrew Marvell, or

Carlyle's "sea-green" Robespierre. Rank as well as wealth might have been his; and the first was repeatedly pressed on him. He spurned both: preferring, as did an Irish member of Parliament of the last century, "to stand well with himself."* A Latin poet has given us a never-failing recipe for gaining the regard of others,—"Love that you may be loved." Mookerjee's unselfishness met with a rich reward; for no modern man of letters ever had a wider circle of devoted friends than he. He was the centre of a group of admiring youths, attracted to him quite as much by his warmth of heart as by the rich stores of learning and observation

* This was Richard Lovell Edgeworth of Edgeworthstown, father of the well-known novelist. When the union of England and Ireland was being prepared for, he was approached by one of Lord Castlereagh's spies in view of securing his vote and interest for the ministerial side. An immense sum of money was offered as a bribe for the betrayal of his country. He refused it, though in sore straits, preferring, as he said, to stand well with himself, *i.e.*, to keep his own self-respect.

which he poured forth to a congenial audience. Nor was his charity confined to his own species. Unmeasured were his denunciations of that passive cruelty which suffers our worn-out drudges to die of slow starvation. When in his daily walks he met a wretched bullock with salient ribs, rough-coat and lack-lustre eye telling of desertion and friendlessness, he always sent it to the Sodpur Pinjrapole. Like Doctor Johnson, of whose portrait as graved deeply by Boswell he reminded one, he was an ardent admirer of "the harmless, necessary cat." His feline pets* were often a dozen or more in

* "My dear Hem Chunder," he writes on the 20th December, 1887,—"Poor Kálay Khan, my grand Bengal Tommy, is dead, I don't know why or how. Could you come and help me to find out by dissection? He was in splendid condition yesterday; but he did not enter appearance at the Cats' Dinner early this morning; nor later, at 2 A.M., when I had my own meal, did he bear me company as usual. At daybreak he was found dead in the yard. I see no blood or other marks of violence on his poor body. You may remember Kálay Khan,

number; and each had its recognised place in his sanctum. The quarrels and jealousies of a specially privileged dog and monkey were subjects of infinite amusement for his friends during his banishment to Eastern Bengal. When they were perforce left behind at Narainganj on his return journey to Calcutta, he presented the boatman who undertook to convey them back to Dacca with a warm overcoat as an inducement to show them every consideration.

Mookerjee's goodness of heart was largely the result of the preponderance of the emotional in his nature. The same characteristic was evinced in his intense appreciation of poetry. His mind was a storehouse of verbal melody :

---

as the black cat, who throve so gloriously. He was, indeed, a grand specimen of the native production, and would be worth stuffing for a museum. I am sorry for the poor creature, whom I loved the more in order to make up for the harshness of others, who despised him because he was black; and they said he was ugly—which last was far from being the case—and persecuted him because he was not as wise as we are."

and he was never so happy as when drinking in inspiration from his favourite bards. Byron was the chief. The wealth of imagery, the burning emotions, the unconquerable love of liberty which find in his stanzas their fittest expression, fascinated my subject. During his stay in Tippera he used to sit up half the night absorbed in "Childe Harold." Once he was moved so deeply by the beauty of the word-painting as to wake up his friend Babu Kumad Nath Banerji and thunder forth the canto beginning:—

> I stood in Venice, on the Bridge of Sighs;
> A palace and a prison on each hand:
> I saw from out the wave her structures rise
> As from the stroke of the enchanter's wand.

The greatest of French novelists, Honoré de Balzac, has said that a craving for posthumous fame is the passion of great spirits just as that for comfort or affluence is the passion of mediocrities. The man of genius who, for his sins, embraces the calling of journalist is debarred from gratifying the "last infirmity of noble minds." His works are written on sand. They deal with ephemeral topics; and they are clean forgotten before the broadsheets which give them to the world are dry. The English custom of anonymity is to blame for this absence of a powerful educer of all that is best in a man: and there are many who think that this drawback outweighs its admitted advantages. A youth who adopts this ungrateful profession must accept the inevitable, and will be fortunate if, by the time he is a grey-headed drudge, his fame is known to the brethren of the quill and midnight oil. The great actor has a more enviable lot. His triumphs are equally evanescent: but then he is sustained by the magnetism of applause, spurred to excel himself by the sympathy of his audience: while the traditions of his feats long survive him. Mookerjee was essentially a journalist; and the fact places his biographer at some disadvantage. For the gentle reader—like Napoleon when the name of a candidate for employ was submitted to him—asks "What has he done?"

It is necessary that I should gratify this very natural curiosity by furnishing extracts from the Doctor's works. But the vast bulk have already appeared in print, and are, from their very nature, unsuited for publication in a permanent form. He has, however, left behind him materials for a volume of original essays. The biography of his colleague Grish Chunder Ghose reveals a marvellous insight into the conditions prevailing in the English Civil Service. The other essays are brimful of his own subtle humour, and illustrate to perfection the quaint antithesis and the apposite quotation in which he took delight.

It is often said that the art of letter-writing is extinct; and, indeed, the spirit of unrest has invaded the scholar's sanctum and robbed him of the mental calm so essential to success in this branch of literature. The letters of our expiring century will be hardly better worth reading than its telegrams. And yet, one cannot guage a writer's claim to originality of mind without studying his private correspondence; really private I mean, not such epistles as Pope's which were evidently written with an eye to publication. But too much must not be expected even from a professed *litterateur*. The anonymous editor of the letters of Bussy-Rabutin (Amsterdam, 1738) puts this very clearly in his preface: "The art of letter-writing is one of the least understood, though nearly every one tries his hand at it: and, what is rather surprizing, professional wits are not by any means the most adept therein. One rarely sees letters from such people couched in a natural and lively style; placing things before a reader much in the same way as they would be put in conversation, and wherein everything is in its place without appearing to be marshalled there by dint of meditation and study. These qualities are much more frequently met within letters written by people whose mental stock-in-trade consists of knowledge of the world, a little reading and a good deal of politeness." Dr. Mookerjee was, perhaps, the antithesis of this ideal letter-writer: but his correspondence is not the less worth perusal. It was carried on with all sorts and conditions of men, and it casts a curious light on the contemporary social history of Calcutta. I have selected some of the most characteristic of his letters which the kindness of his friends has placed at my disposal. In comparatively rare cases have communications addressed to him been reprinted. There are, indeed, few readers who would not have enjoyed the complete correspondence which passed between my subject and the Marquis of Dufferin, Sir Auckland Colvin and Sir Charles Elliott. It is greatly to the credit of these statesmen that they should have maintained friendly and even confidential relations with an obscure man of letters, but the time has not yet come when opinions expressed in unguarded intercourse should be given to the world. Apart from the breach of confidence involved, a literary executor must bear in mind the advice given by Louis XIV. of France to a volatile relative. The king remarked that the lightest words of men of their rank were more pregnant than the weightiest ones of ordinary people.

If, in spite of many inevitable omissions, my sketch should reveal to Mookerjee's countrymen a curious and, indeed, unique personality, and lessen the prejudices entertained by so many Englishmen against the community from which he sprang, my labour of love will not have been in vain.

CORRESPONDENCE

OF

DR. SAMBHU C. MOOKERJEE.

CORRESPONDENCE.

From Major Evans Bell.

Nagpur, August 11, 1860.

Dear Sir,—Your letter of the 5th ultimo has remained unanswered for this most unreasonable period, partly on account of an attack of illness, and partly from my time and attention being somewhat closely and unpleasantly occupied during the last fortnight. I was very glad indeed to see the two petitions, for which I return you my best thanks. The case for the exemption of Zemindars under the Permanent Settlement is very ably stated ; but I confess it has only confirmed me in my opinion that they have no valid case for exemption from any general tax.

Upon the Income Tax itself I look with horror ; it is a crude, ill-considered measure and comes down far too low in the scale of society. It will work most cruelly, and I believe the collections will be much less than are expected.

It is probable that I may be at Calcutta about the end of September, when I should like very much to make your personal acquaintance.

Believe me faithfully yours,

EVANS BELL.

The succeeding letter was written in reply to one from Doctor Mookerjee enclosing a review of Sir W. W. Hunter's *Dictionary of the non-Aryan Languages.*

From Mr. W. W. Hunter.

Stamp Office, Calcutta, June 21, 1861.

My dear Sir,—I received your letter with much pleasure. The review of the Dictionary was an excellent one. I have never sought praise at the hands of any one, only truth ; and some of your hints are most valuable.

I think you could not have had the Dissertation with you when you ascribe to it any imputation against the Hindus. I most carefully guard against such a mistake by saying that the conduct of a few aggressors in no way tells against the honour of a nation. If it did, what a tale could be told about England! But a nation with the instinct of conquest cannot help itself. It can only do justice and shew mercy as it goes along. The man who draws a picture of the spread of Aryan civilization in India in ancient times will confer a benefit on the whole Indo-Germanic stock. Why not attempt it? You have got great advantages for such a task.

Yours sincerely,

W. W. HUNTER.

Babu Dakhinaranjan Mookerjee, to whom the following letter is addressed, was a person who made a considerable stir in his day, as the mainspring of the Oudh Taluqdars' Association, of which Dr. Mookerjee became Assistant Secretary. The introductory memoir (p. 25) gives particulars of the work done by our hero for that body. Subsequent communications between them are couched in a different tone. Dr. Mookerjee was unable to obtain his arrears of salary; and it is rather entertaining to observe the changes of mood through which his impressionable mind passed as the sense of injury, of ingratitude and of undeserved poverty came uppermost. It is, however, best that such correspondence should pass into oblivion.

To Baboo Dakhinaranjan Mookerjee,

Honorary Secretary to the British Indian Association, Oudh, Lucknow, Oudh.

May, 1863.

Sir,—I have the honour to inform you that circumstances have called me home, and as I do not expect to return to Lucknow, I hereby resign my post as Assistant Secretary to the British Indian Association of Oudh and Editor of its English newspaper *Samachar Hindustani*, and beg you will have the goodness to accept my resignation.

It is more than a year since I took charge of my duties. During that period I am conscious of occasional acts of carelessness, and I owe you thanks for having generously forgiven them. On the whole, however, I have tried to perform my duties as well as my time and ability permitted. In that, I trust, I have succeeded.

Of my management of the newspaper I am not the best judge, and indeed intellectual labour is such a subtle thing that it is not easy to demonstrate that a labourer in that field has done his duty. I can, therefore, only hope that I have done mine. Of one thing, however, I can speak with more certainty, because the proofs seem incontestible. I have greatly raised the position of the paper from what it was. When I took charge of it, the *Samachar Hindustani* was noticed by other papers only with contempt, but within a month of my taking charge it began to be treated with consideration, and I have the happiness of leaving it in the full enjoyment of public respect. It is now quoted both in India and England and alluded to by the Viceroy and the Secretary of State. Even a political opponent, Mr. Laing, whom we have so often exposed, certainly in no hesitating spirit, feels it necessary to propitiate us in his last pamphlet by praising the "great moderation and ability" with which the *Samachar Hindustani* is conducted. I do not mention these results in any unworthy spirit of vanity; but it is impossible that I should not feel a legitimate pride when I think of them. I do not say that there was no room for improvement. Far from it. I am but too conscious of the deficiencies of the paper; but I am as far from feeling ashamed of the position in which, all circumstances considered, I leave it. It also gives me pleasure to feel that, while you are the Honorary Secretary of the Association, the paper cannot fall into unworthy hands. Indeed, I am certain that my successor, whoever he may be, will be worthier of it than I have proved myself to be.

I freely acknowledge the able and obliging assistance which I have always received from my valued contributors. Nor can I omit to mention the aid which the paper received from your suggestions and the moderation of your counsels.

Accept my thanks for all the kindness which, in your official position or in private life, I have received at your hands; and allow me to hope that, although I leave the service of the Association and the Province, you will continue to be a friend and patron to

Your obedient servant,

SAMBHU C. MOOKERJEE.

The Doctor's correspondent in the following communication was destined to earlier fame than attends most Anglo-Indians. He was at this time busy with his colossal "Gazetteer of India." One of the leading features in his scheme for writing the district annals of Bengal was to secure the co-operation of local antiquarians and native chroniclers. Hence his preference for men over books as sources of information.

From Mr. W. W. Hunter.

The Grange, Alderley, Walton-under-Edge,
Gloucestershire, October 26, 1868.

Dear Sir,—Kindly insert the enclosed advertisement in your paper. The work which it announces is already published in England, and as soon as I can secure a copy one will be forwarded for your acceptance.

I have made it a rule never to address an editor on his review of my book. But your elaborate criticism of my *Annals of Rural Bengal* tempts me to depart from the resolution. Your discriminating remarks gave me more pleasure than if you had merely repeated the praises of the English, French and American reviewers. But I could not help regretting that you slightly misconceived the purpose of my book. It would have been easy enough for me to have filled it with antiquarian details such as you set forth, for I have several trunks of manuscripts on these subjects, but it would have destroyed the character of my undertaking. My object is to interpret the people of India to the English nation. At present, the Indian races justly complain that they are not realized by the governing body and that we fail to take that interest which it is our duty to show in Indian affairs. In this object the *Annals* have succeeded beyond my hopes. It is the only book on India that has run through three editions and been reprinted in America within four months of its publication. I am writing for your own eye, and I mention these circumstances only to add that I value them as nothing compared with the co-operation and hearty sympathy of the natives of India. I have taken as the work of my life the interpretation of your countrymen to my own and my success must depend, not upon a flourish of trumpets at setting out, but upon the support of that community which you represent. I am at the beginning of an enterprise in which my most valuable co-adjutors must be not books but men.

I am, yours truly,

W. W. HUNTER.

From Mr. W. W. Hunter.

Oakwood, Simla, July 16, 1871.

My dear Sir,—I have just received your note of the 12th and shall be very glad to see your recently published work. I have heard it very favourably spoken of, and perhaps if you let me know the Indian papers which have not noticed it, I might be able to help you in the matter of review. Has the *Englishman* or the *Pioneer* taken it up?

I am glad to see that you are determined to go on in the literary vocation. When I reflect how difficult I should find it to write a book in a foreign language, I admire and honour the gentlemen of Bengal who have so thoroughly mastered my own.

I am, yours faithfully,

W. W. HUNTER.

From Major Evans Bell.

37, Holland Villas Road,
Kensington, W., October 20, 1871.

My dear Sir,—For the last month I have been travelling about, as so many of us do in this country at this time of year, and only returned home about a week ago. This will plead as my excuse for not having before this replied to your letter of the 5th August, which has only been in my hands for about a fortnight, as we were for some weeks beyond the reach of the post. I am very glad, indeed, to renew communications and greetings with you, although we have never met in the flesh. I well remember your pamphlet on Mr. Wilson and the Income Tax, and your receiving in good part some strictures I volunteered on what I ventured to think were some superfluous personalities in it,—an error of style into which I had been too prone to fall myself. But you undoubtedly fastened on the right subject, and the monstrous extravagance of the expenditure and blundering severities of the fiscal expedients that have since been the chief characteristics of our financial policy, have amply justified the note of alarm that you sounded at so early a period.

We are really doing good work at the centre of Imperial Government here with the East India Association, which daily gains accessions of influential members, and wins its way as a recognized authority. I regret to see the small amount, comparatively speaking, of support which it meets with at Calcutta. I was sorry to hear that it is a common saying even among some of the Hindu gentlemen in London from your Provinces,—"Oh, it is quite a Bombay concern!"—which is probably reflected back to Bengal and checks your sympathies. If the greater part of our subscriptions comes from Bombay, that is due to the energy of our noble Honorary Secretary Dadabhai Naoroji, and can easily be counterbalanced if some of the Bengali members will make equal efforts in their localities. But that the attention of the Association is chiefly or to any special extent given to Bombay topics is quite untrue, as our proceedings will testify. You may have recently observed the splendid donation of half a lakh of rupees that has been made by the Maha Rao of Kutch, which may be said to ensure the permanence of the Association, but we cannot attain the fullest possible degree of efficiency and usefulness without a good list of subscribers and correspondents in Bengal. If your politicians devote themselves too exclusively to local interests, they will never secure general co-operation in the highest objects of their political action.

Provincial selfishness and sectarian jealousy will always defeat themselves. I cannot forget that, until almost the last struggle, the Bengali papers gave scanty aid to the fight in favour of the Mysore State,—and for the most part they sneered at the claims of the Nawab of the Carnatic. And even in a case that might be supposed to come closer to them, that of the Nawab Nazim of Bengal, I don't observe that the educated and enlightened Bengalis make the slightest demonstration on the side of good faith and honesty. Depend on it that is the point to decide, and the only one worth deciding,—has the case the balance of justice and truth on its side? Is the faith of Government pledged or not? Once permit the Government to diverge, unquestioned and unchallenged, from the path of honour and fair dealing, for the sake of some temporary advantage or mere material saving, and none of you are safe. If you Bengalis, from want of personal or class interest in the affairs of a great Mussulman family, permit the spoliation and disinheritance of the Nawab Nazim's heirs to be effected without remonstrance, some day or other short work will be made of the Permanent Settlement. But perhaps you don't care for the Settlement or the Zemindars. I don't; but I care very much for the plighted faith of our Government.

I like your books very much, and shall take much interest in your future work. I shall always be glad to hear from you.

Believe me, sincerely yours,

EVANS BELL.

From Major Evans Bell.

37, Holland Villas Road,
Kensington, W., London, October 31, 1872.

Dear Sir,—I am afraid I shall never lack an excuse for delaying to reply to a letter, but I really have put off answering yours of the 10th ultimo until I had first been to Paternoster Row and secured the copies of *Mookerjee's Magazine* which you so kindly forwarded to me. Indeed, on returning home and referring to your letter, I find I have appropriated No. 3 (which had been just received at Trübner's) of which you made no mention to me, inasmuch as it was not published when you wrote. Of course, I might have written to Mr. Trübner and have asked him to send me the Magazines; but then you see I should have lost a good excuse for delay which has lasted me for a fortnight. I have always more writing engagements than I can easily fulfil, and for the last nine months I have had a succession of family troubles and complications—chiefly arising from the dangerous illness and disordered affairs of my father-in-law, which have given me much work and anxiety. I have been much interested in all that I have as yet had time to read in your Magazine,—particularly in your political reflections called forth in commenting on the career of your friend Grish Chunder Ghose. I do not think I ever read anything of his. Why do you say in your letter to me, that, since Lord Lawrence became Viceroy, the policy of Government has been repressive and retrograde—"openly and insultingly so?" I am dying for facts. You will see by the paper which I read a few months ago before the East India Association that I am conscious of the unimproved—to say the least—spirit of our administration, here at the India Office and at Calcutta, but I want facts.

For example, I am told by Engineer officers here (even by Sir Arthur Cotton, who is in many respects a liberal man,) that there are no Hindu Engineers, and no promising pupils available,—that natives, especially of Bengal, are physically unfit for exposure to the sun, for travelling long distances, and, of course, the old story of their being morally untrustworthy, both for the disbursement of money and for the conscientious supervision of work. Now, I don't want recrimination and exposure of the shortcomings of English officers, except to supplement and illustrate facts proving the capabilities of Native Engineers—and so in other Departments also. You know, and may see by the accompanying paper, that I will speak out, but I must have facts to give weight to my assertions. I am astonished that so little remonstrance has come from India with regard to the Cooper's Hill College,—the most monstrous and cruel job that has been perpetrated for many years. I fastened on it at once in *Public*

Works and Public Service in India, published last year. As you may possibly not have seen this, I send you a copy by post. My paper read at the East India Association is not yet published in the journal, so that the full discussion that followed does not appear in the proof now sent. You may have observed that our indefatigable Dadabhai Naoroji has secured for the East India Association several contributions from Native Princes (the last being Rs. 25,000 from Holkar,) which go very far to make the institution permanent and self-supporting. His efforts in this direction, both here and in India, have cost him a great deal of money and have so much diverted his attention from his commercial affairs * * * * that his interests have suffered severely. Yet I hear that he has scruples as to accepting the post of paid Secretary on his return to London—hitherto the office has been honorary,—for fear it should be thought that such was his object in obtaining donations and subscriptions. We shall, however, bring great pressure to bear upon him, when he arrives here, to compel him to take the place, for which no one else is equally competent, and to which no one can have so good a title. But, though the Association is undoubtedly doing good, we are terribly in want of Parliamentary support. There is after all no power in the Association, except such as we can exercise through the few members of Parliament who attend our meetings and whom we can set in motion. But there is a great lack of boldness and independence among them. That noble and intrepid champion, Mr. Fawcett, who so wonderfully surmounts the limits and obstacles of his sad infirmity,—though still kept by it within a comparatively narrow circle,—stands almost alone in the House. And unless a man possesses the vantage-ground of a seat in Parliament, the right of being heard and the right of insisting on information and answer to enquiries that a

Member of the House of Commons holds, he feels a hundred times every session that with all his knowledge and all the energy of conviction and prevision, he is practically impotent. No one out of the House of Commons, or without the public mission conferred by a seat there, can speak with authority, or make himself heard beyond the walls of a lecture-room. I always speak with restraint and reserve, because I feel that the full truth would be thrown away or misinterpreted before what can only be considered a private audience.

I will do my best to make your literary venture known here. Have you sent any copies to any of the London Press? I would recommend the *Examiner* and the *Asiatic*.

With kind regards,

Believe me, sincerely yours,

EVANS BELL.

The person to whom the next letter was addressed was one of the most regular and by no means the least brilliant contributors to *Mookerjee's Magazine.* His sketches of military life, with its lights and shadows impartially displayed, richly merit reprinting.

To Captain T. O. Underwood.

(Rajanpur, Dira Ghazikhan, the Punjab.)

Calcutta, August 20, 1874.

My dear Sir,—I have just received yours of the 13th instant acknowledging receipt of the first half of a hundred rupee note. The other half I have the pleasure to post to-day.

Yesterday I posted your MS. of the "Frontier Officer." Those copies of the issue in which "The S. Subaltern" appears will be duly forwarded to you.

Two copies of the number containing the "Frontier Officer" have, I believe, been sent—one to your address, and another to that of Mrs. Underwood.

Let the Brahman go hanged! I don't care, I mean, let him be represented in fiction just as authors choose, or find convenient for purposes of the unities, or interest or sensation.

I am sure I can enjoy a laugh against my own people. Even a dead set, if enlivened by wit and humour, or characterized by unusual skill, I can admire on artistic grounds, though I may be opposed to it on others. Art is Art, Literature, Literature. And your literary presentation of any topic is yours, not mine. It is well understood that I do not write the whole Magazine, nor do I hold myself responsible for every social or political opinion that appears in it. The Magazine was indeed started as an organ of opinion of all classes, and, had I been supported by writers who differ from me in faith, politics and literary views, it might have earned that character. Now it has certainly got into a particular party groove ; and I, of course, try to give the opinions appearing in it a certain unity of character. Still, where the subject and circumstances admit of such a course—where, that is, the writing is not likely to be much confounded with my own, I allow the expression of others' opinion. It is on this principle I have printed the paper "The English," in which the writer has, in my opinion, failed to enter into the spirit of the disguise he has put on. The opinions therein expressed are those of an observant Englishman who has not penetrated into the depths of our society, who, if he speaks at all like a native, speaks like one of those uneducated native youths who, ignorant of their own society and of the world, have been dazzled by the external aspects and advantages of English life at Home. He has perhaps been made a small lion of. Some of the very points in English school and college life which are recommended to our admiration, have been condemned by thoughtful writers like Mr. Thomas Hughes and others—the universal bullying and tyrannizing of the strong over the weak which are such bugbears to the sensitive and delicately organized, the undue encouragement of boat races and such like athletic rather than simply manly sports, &c. Then the mother's solicitude for the health, the personal appearance and the spiritual welfare of her young hopeful, the scrubbing, dressing, kneeling at prayers, &c., are represented as peculiarly English phenomena. In truth, they are universal—descending down to the "beasts that perish." There is, doubtless, some difference in the results of English and Indian maternal care—from the difference of education, &c., between the mothers of the two races. But as yet the English mater-familias is not so far advanced as to make the difference in favour of English children so very striking as Englishmen might think, or an Indian who has "seen the world" of Europe. In spite of the father and the physician, the English mother is as prone as her enlightened Hindu or Moslem sister to drug her children —with equal results. But enough. I write all this from no feeling of irritation, I assure you, but just to vindicate my catholicity and ease of temper, my spirit of toleration, indifferentism if you will. I have even allowed the statement to stand that "the English are fast making us rich," though that is matter for doubt, and involves a large politico-economical question, which I am prepared to argue at a suitable time and place. There is an article in the number in the press on Indian Commerce in which you will get an inkling of our views. I have taken the liberty of altering the passage on the Brahmos in "The English," in accordance with our opinion. * * * *

All this *en passant* as a preliminary to my request to let me see "The Nana" of which I have been dreaming so long. Up to this moment I have heard nothing to lead me to suppose I should not publish it. All I care is, it must be a hit, be it at the expense of all the Brahmans in the world. You seem to think that Brahmans are all the Hindus. It is true, I am a Brahman—the bluest of the blue, lineally and purely descended, as I am taught to believe by our Heralds' College, through the entire Pantheon from great Brahmá himself and

Brahma itself (" Brahmá " and " Brahma " are very different things—so much lies in the turn of a single vowel)—and, of course, as great a *Budmash* as your Muse may regard one—I am something more than a Brahman—that is, a child of Western culture, an humble admirer of the European Muses, who esteems Shakespeare above Kalidasa and all the poets that have been or probably shall be.

Not that I have no strong opinions, no earnest partialities. On the contrary, all these with me are very strong and earnest, but still not too much so for toleration and temper. And I may as well tell you that the Nana is not my weakness. What is that bloated Mahratta fellow to me? If I really thought well of the historical Nana, I would not be afraid to say so above my name in print, but the fellow was a worthless wretch who spoilt his cause by his crimes. But diabolical as they were, they do not affect his countrymen any more than Sumroo's affect Europeans. The

Brahman business of your play will not in the least detract from its merit in my eyes either as critic, man, Hindu, Brahman or editor of *Mookerjee's Magazine*. So you may go on piling the agony on your miscreant—who appears to be the hero of your work. As good a hero as you could get, perhaps, in an age in which "every year and month sends forth a new one."* You have the high authority of Milton on your side, the real hero of Paradise Lost being Satan. But as a critic, I may be permitted to suggest that there ought to be light as well as shade in your picture. Who is the heroine? She may be taken from among the fair European victims of 1857, but for purposes of art—even sensational art—there ought to be a foil of goodness even in the native camp to the hideousness

* I want a hero: an uncommon want,
When every year and month sends forth a new one,
Till, after cloying the gazettes with cant,
The age discovers he is not the true one.
BYRON.

of its chief the Nana. The English public, I apprehend, will not at this late hour appreciate all the evil being shown on one side. I believe it is an intellectual necessity to have some good spirits about Nana—one or two—to thwart his purposes, to bring out the plot, delay the catastrophe. His mother must be made motherly, to arouse indignation against the unnatural conduct of her son ; and so of his sisters. But these are truisms. It seems I cannot write a letter of moderate dimensions when I am in the mood.

So, then, send me The Nana—also the Dak Bungalow Military Traveller.

The S. S. appears in the forthcoming number.

It is sometimes hard to pass your writing properly through the press owing to my want of familiarity with all the slang and allusions of Anglo-Indian military life. Thus, I left the last word in the "Frontier Officer" as I found it, "siller," without comprehending what it means. Generally, as you may have remarked, I get on well enough, and, what is more, enjoy the jokes —which is more than the best educated among us can say always.

My health is somewhat better now, thank you.

Yours truly,

SAMBHU C. MOOKERJEE.

To Captain T. O. Underwood.

4th Punjab Cavalry,

Rajanpore, Punjab Frontier.

August 31, 1874.

My dear Sir,—I have received yours of the 21st from Rajanpore and of the 24th from Hurrund Dak Bungalow. I believe I acknowledged your previous notes.

I do not want the "Bostan" and will also take the liberty to return the "Pestilence" which, for one reason, is out of season. Altogether, I do not require the verses, having a good supply at home.

It will be necessary to secure the copyright of the Nana for England by special steps as the law directs, to prevent its being pirated by unprincipled printers. I will write to enquire.

Your cover encloses a new commencement for the Dak Bungalow. I shall put it in the proper place.

I have recovered, thank you.

I wish you a pleasant trip and a safe return to your Regiment at Rajanpore. I fear your journey will not be unattended with peculiar dangers. I have no information about the Beluchis in particular, but the frontier tribes are generally regarded as tough customers and inconvenient neighbours. Many have been the Englishmen murdered by vindictive Wuziris, Bunnus, Afghans. During Sir John Lawrence's administration of India, the Punjab Government got a summary law passed to check these outrages. Of course, their frequency was much exaggerated; and on that ground, but chiefly on general principles of legislation, I thought it my duty to oppose the Bill through the press. Still there is no doubt of the turbulence and recklessness of life of the people to the West of the Punjab. A Frontier officer, civil or military, has to be very careful indeed, and he must be a man of pluck and presence of mind and quickness of perception, if not of daring. It must be a fine school, the Frontier. Nowhere is there so much need for patience, self-respect, charity, respect for others' feelings, even tenderness towards strange prejudices. The Briton cannot find a better place for quickly having his swagger and bluster, and snobbery and hauteur, and undisguised contempt for other races (European not excepted) knocked out of his head. Great temper, tact and judgment must be required in dealing with the strong, death-despising, short-tempered natives on the Frontier. To my mind, there is no discipline like spending a few years there.

But why am I boring you with all this nonsense? What need to ship coals to Newcastle?

To us stay-at-homes of Bengal, the idea of a

civilized man travelling amid the sands and rocks bordering on Beluchistan, inspecting the British out-posts, has something curious about it.

Perhaps, this long yarn, if it does reach you there, from one whose face is dark and of whom, such as he is, you have no idea, may be a moment's consolation and occupation. It is because it may be so, that I have allowed myself to fill the whole sheet. A letter going so far ought to be made worth carrying so far. The same half anna will carry a long letter as a short one.

Yours most sincerely,
SAMBHU C. MOOKERJEE.

To Nawab Sir Salar Jung Bahadar, K.C.S.I., Minister-Regent of Hyderabad.

Tivoli Gardens.

Calcutta, January 8, 1875.

May it please your Excellency,—According to the custom of the country, I beg to approach your Excellency with my humble *nuzzer*. My ancestors, the sages and philosophers of old used to greet kings and ministers with their blessings and a worn-out *pothi* or two. A degenerate descendant of theirs, but a humble seeker of knowledge and in a way imparter too, I welcome to my country the great Minister-Regent of the Kingdom of the Deccan with my best prayers to the Almighty for his prosperity, temporal and spiritual, and, for my nuzzer, offer for his kind acceptance all I can afford in the shape of two or three tracts, namely, "The Prince in India and to India, by a Native of India," being an account of the visit of His Royal Highness the Duke of Edinburgh, and two numbers of a periodical of which I have the honour to be editor, *Mookerjee's Magazine.* I wish I could add a copy of some of my other separate small publications, such as "The Career of an Indian Princess—the late Begum Sekundra of Bhopal", which the London *Spectator* in a long editorial review characterized, among other things, as the work of "a shrewd hard-hitting critic with no small political ability." That paper, indeed, is somewhat partial, though outspoken enough to my humble lucubrations, as I hear it also noticed favourably "The Prince in India," though I did not read the notice myself.

I have been connected with the Indian Press for the last 18 years, though comparatively unknown myself, because writing anonymously. So long ago as 1857, a pamphlet of mine appeared in London entitled "Causes of the Mutiny by a Hindu of Bengal." With an Introduction by Malcolm Lewin, Esq., late a Judge of the Madras Court of Judicature, Author of numerous Tracts on India. It failed of its due effect because, as Mr. Lewin informed me, few in those days were aware of the progress English education had made in India, or could believe it was the work of a genuine native of India: and as many disliked Mr. Lewin for his rather extreme views, there were not wanting people so unjust to him to hint that the Hindu was a mythical character of his own creation, though there were in the ideas of my essays and in some of the very idioms (for I was a very young writer then, still pursuing my studies at college,) unmistakable evidence of a native Indian origin. In the discussion of the Income Tax when it was first proposed by the late Right Honourable James Wilson, I put forth a pamphlet, the needless personalities of which were universally condemned, but the force of its arguments were acknowledged by many candid critics in Bengal.

I was associated, equally with my friend Babu Kristodas Pal, editor of the *Hindoo Patriot*, who has at length received some of his due by being called to the Legislative Council of Bengal—first with the editor of the *Hindoo Intelligencer*, the late Babu Kashiprasad Ghosh, author of the Shair and other poems, &c., the first successful writer of English poetry among the natives of India, and then with the first editor of the *Hindoo Patriot*, the lamented

Babu Hurish Chunder Mookerjee, in the conduct of the respective journals. On the death of the latter, I was appointed his successor. Giving up that charge in consequence of a fundamental difference of political views with an influential section, I went to Oudh as paid Secretary of the Taluqdars' Association and editor of their English organ with the queer Hindustani name, the *Samachar Hindustani* (since incorporated with the *Oudh Gazette* and subsequently the *Lucknow Times.*) Your Excellency may possibly remember the *Samachar* as about the only paper that defended your master His Highness the late Nizamul Mulk Afzuluddaula Bahadur and the late Colonel Davidson, then Resident, from the storm raised against them by the Indian press and public regarding the presentation to, and reception by, the Ruler of the Deccan of the Insignia of the Star of India—certainly the only paper that, without any personal interest in the matter or communication with Hyderabad, was active in the defence, and tried to lay before the public the true bearings of the case. The defence led me into some hot controversy with other papers, but I am so proud of the part I took in it, that I have yet thoughts, under suitable encouragement, of reprinting the articles I wrote, with a selection of others of my anonymous essays in a separate form.

The Hon'ble Samuel Laing, successor to the late Mr. Wilson, though I had often enough occasion to expose with sharpness what I deemed his fallacies, had the generosity to record in his pamphlet on India and China his opinion of my journal as one "conducted with great ability and moderation."

In the intervals of my journalistic career, I have assisted Native Chiefs called to the Viceroy's Council for making laws, or been at Native Courts like those of Murshidabad and Rampur. Some years before the Nawab Nazim of Bengal went to Europe, I was appointed his Personal Assistant and subsequently was entrusted with the entire charge of his affairs, which I managed until I resigned in disgust at the intrigues of the opposition and being latterly inadequately supported by the Prince. His Highness the Nawab of Rampur was pleased to call me to his Court as his Secretary, and I might have remained there but for my personal friendship with his brother Nawab Hyder Ali Khan with whom I became acquainted when at Murshidabad, which he had once visited on the occasion of the Beara Festival and where he had made a stay of a few weeks. The Chief became jealous of his brother's kindness for me, and conveyed to me a hint of his displeasure at my visit to Nawab Hyder Ali Khan Bahadur. As a gentleman I could not give up an old friend, but I assured His Highness that such a step on my part would not be necessary as he would find me faithful to the "salt." Perhaps, this fact may be some recommendation of me to your Excellency's kindness, as I understand that you were kind to Nawab

Hyder Ali Khan himself. But though I thus left Rampur, His Highness otherwise behaved very kindly towards me, and has done so since, in that he sent a handsome donation towards the expenses of "The Prince," when the Prospectus was sent to him by the Publishers.

Since then I have been associated with the present editor of the *Hindoo Patriot*, in which, besides literary and social subjects, my special department is that of extra-Bengal affairs and Foreign Policy.

I am now engaged on the conduct of my own *Mookerjee's Magazine*.

This periodical has a double character—first that of a non-exclusive liberal Indian literary journal open to all races, creeds and parties, through which civil, military and non-official European writers, address the public. Several brilliant military sketches have lately appeared in its pages, such as "The Battle of Donkeying—a View of Modern Warfare by an ancient British Man of War", "Episodes in a

Military Life," the last being the first paper of a series to appear from time to time. In the double number sent herewith, there is the conclusion of "The Dak Bungalow—a military story." There is also the first part of an elaborate essay, "On the Obstacles to the Introduction of Christianity in India" intended for a London Quarterly, in which the writer propounds novel and bold views. The second character of the Magazine is that of the only organ, in all India, of the most advanced native culture and aspirations.

Such a publication could hardly fail to give offence in many quarters, but among its contributors figure such names as the late Justice Dwarka Nath Mitter (of the High Court in Bengal), the late Babu Grish Chunder Ghose (editor of the *Bengalee*), the late Michael M. S. Datta (Barrister-at-Law, author of "The Captive Ladie" and other poems, the great Bengali poet and dramatist), Raja Jotindra Mohun Tagore, the Revd. K. M. Banerjee, Dr. Rajendralala Mitra, Babu O. C. Dutt, (Vice-Chairman of the Calcutta Municipality), and many others whose names I am not permitted to give, besides the European writers alluded to above.

* * * *

With many apologies for trespassing so much on your valuable time,

I have the honour to remain,

Your Excellency's most obedient servant,

Sambhu C. Mookerjee.

To Sir T. Madhava Rao,

Prime Minister of the State of Baroda.

1, Wellington Square,

Calcutta, September 22, 1875.

Sir,—I must apologise for addressing direct so exalted a person as you are, but considering my errand, I could hardly, with satisfaction to both sides, betake to any other course.

I feel that, as editor of *Mookerjee's Magazine*, which has condemned the policy of our Government in Baroda affairs, I may be thought to commit an impropriety or to evince a want

8

of delicacy in addressing the statesman charged with the carrying out of the supplementary measures in that policy. In that feeling I have hesitated for over a month and half. If there was any valid objection at any time, that time, I hope, has long passed away, and I may now venture on a task otherwise so grateful. In passing I would remark that we all—Young India as we are all called, though some of us are old enough by this—acknowledge our unfeigned gratitude to the Power which gives us protection, which has taught us the value of constitutional liberty, which allows us the freedom of our thoughts and aspirations, as we acknowledge our obligation to render it every legitimate service, whether we have or have not any honest doubts as to the wisdom of resolution or step taken by it, indeed even though we may have considered it our duty to oppose that step in a constitutional way.

I have long perceived that the absence of works of reference is much in the way of Englishmen here or at home taking an interest in or comprehending the affairs of this country. These can never be comprehended without some mastery of the places and persons in question. It is difficult under any circumstances for Europeans to master the names, but the difficulty is heightened by the absence of information available to the public in a convenient shape. This absence is not only in the way of Europeans desiring to know the East, but also in that of the natives themselves. I have frequently had occasion in writing of the affairs of Native States in the *Hindoo Patriot* to bewail the want of information exhibited by the Indian Press and generally the ignorance of India regarding herself. I have indeed long meditated a Peerage of India, a Knightage, a Manual of the Native States and a Dictionary of Contemporary Oriental Biography containing every Asiatic name of note. The proposals of the last were published by my publishers, and the undertaking recommended in a leading article in the *Patriot.*

No adequate encouragement being received, the work was not persevered in, though I have got the materials in great part ready. I have thought that the visit of his Royal Highness the Prince of Wales may be a favourable time for bringing these or some of these out. I would respectfully solicit not only such patronage of the Baroda State as you may think fit to grant but also your valuable co-operation in supplying information regarding the State with which you have been or are connected and your ownself.

I shall feel much obliged if you will be kind enough to order a statement to be furnished to me of the constitution and *personnel* of administration of Baroda with the duties and salaries attached, and a column noting the antecedents and former services of the several officers.

Besides the separate publications, I intend

to publish a series of biographies, in as much detail as I can gather, of our most prominent native statesmen. I could not commence with a more brilliant example than the present minister of Baroda. May I request the favour of any particulars you may think proper to communicate regarding yourself beyond those given in Mr. Norton's *Topics?* I need scarcely say that the communications will be held strictly confidential.

Begging your pardon for this liberty of a perfect stranger,

I subscribe myself, with great respect, Sir,

Your most obedient servant,

SAMBHU C. MOOKERJEE.

To Dr. Rajendralala Mitra.

1, Wellington Square,

Calcutta, February 28, 1876.

My dear Rajendra,—I am thinking of your last evening's request to help you to any traces of human sacrifice I may have met with in the course of my reading.

The custom seems to have been universal, not only in the earliest stage of savagery of all races, but even at a comparatively advanced period of semi-barbarism.

I dare say you have hunted up all the traces in Sanskrit literature and in our own country, and made inferences from apparently irrelevant matter.

That story of the Indian Hatem, Karna the Liberal, plainly speaks of a period when human flesh was esteemed a delicacy.

I don't believe, at least don't just now remember, that the Rajputs destroy their infant daughters on any pretence of making a sacrifice to the gods or the devil, as in the throwing of children to the sea.

The Indian custom may be traced in the Bible. You will recall Abraham's offer of Isaac. There is another remarkable vow which it is sought to explain away as only meaning the dedication to God of the person of a daughter who was kept a virgin in consequence, but which really was a vow for offering up a human life.

It is long since I read Burton's and Forbes' books on Dahomey and don't remember what sort of religious rites, if any, are connected with the sanguinary practices of that formidable kingdom.

The sacrifice prevailed among the ancient Americans—the Incas, Aztecs, and others as well as among the later tribes with whom the Europeans came in contact. There have been of late years some good works on Peruvian and other American antiquities. There is no doubt that on the occasion of the four chief festivals of the Peruvians held in the four seasons, it was no unusual thing to sacrifice a beautiful boy or girl, perhaps one of the "virgins of the sun." As the Incas, the civilizers of the South American aborigines, were a particularly mild and inoffensive race, it is probable that this was a relic of an ancient popular superstition, once more freely indulged in and permitted by the new rulers in deference to the wishes of their subjects.

Similarly, the "civilized" Aztecs of the North, with all their comparative refinement, were addicted at once to human sacrifice in their temples and cannibalism at their tables.

Mr. Heaviside, in his *American Antiquities or the New World and the Old and the Old World and the New*, quotes a myth in the sacred book of the Taltec race in America regarding two hero gods who were burnt and their ashes thrown into the water, and the hero-gods rising on the fifth day—which seems to me to refer to a human sacrifice.

It is difficult in India to find the books you want. Doubtless, the Asiatic Society's Library contains some which will be useful to you, and for others you may try the Calcutta Public Library. The Dutt Family collection is in wretched disorder and a great many volumes are missing. You will, at any rate, easily procure the charming works of Prescott.

I have read of them in reviews and so forth, but never come across Thatcher's Indian Biography and M'Kenny and Hall's History of the Indian Tribes of North America. If you can procure them, will you lend them to me for a while? Herodotus is a storehouse of many strange, antique and savage customs.

The Scandinavians offered up human lives to Thor, Woden and Frea. Professor Holmboe delights to trace coincidences between Eastern and Western ways. The identifier of Buddha and Woden and the phallic worship of the East and the West, may have noticed the similarity between the human sacrifice of India and that of his own part of the globe. But you are more familiar with his writings, having been the first to popularize, through the medium of English, his speculations on the traces of Buḍdhism in Europe.

See if Jenning's trashy book on the Roscicrucians, my copy of which is at Baranagore, contains any reference to your subject. Also Inman's *Ancient Faiths.*

The Druids and Saxons, I believe, habitually offered human sacrifices. In fact, the orgies and rites in the temples of Sweden and Denmark were repeated in the caves of Britain. Like the demonaic Tantric devotees of India, the priests of the barbarians of Northern Europe were themselves the butchers. So the Galims among the Tipperas.

I need not refer to the authorities for the rites and practices of Old Egypt, Assyria, Greece, Persia, &c, in fact of Northern Africa, Eastern Europe and Western Asia—any more than to Sanskrit or other Indian materials, towards an account of human sacrifice as practised in all ages.

The Meriah sacrifices, &c., are notorious. *Narabali* is a well-known thing among Hindus, and was habitually indulged in by tribes and sects.

The Thugs gave a religious air to their terrible trade.

I should not wonder if the Dyaks of Borneo so famous for head-hunting, and the natives of Australasia for cannibalism, imparted a religious mysticism to their respective pastimes and feats.

Boyle's works on Borneo, published, I believe, in 1865, represent the head-hunting as a rather decaying custom. Probably, it is in full force still in the far moffussil.

Against those uncompromising champions of Holy Writ, or rather of the children of Israel as an all-worthy people, and of their neighbours in general as respectable persons, I may mention that within this century the modern Jews in their own Holy Land and the countries adjacent have been accused of not scrupling to take human life in pursuit of a mistaken religious object. I should not wonder if they are still charged with the same practices. At least I read that, during the reign of Sultan Mahmood, in the Turkish Empire, one sect of Jews kidnapped Christian children and put them to a horrible death for the "love of God." The unfortunate victims were rolled within barrels the inside of which is spiked all over with sharp nails and pins. To prevent their making any noise, their tongues were first cut out. The blood was used for communion. This astounding savagery was committed (it was said) in view of a passage in the Gospel wherein Christ tells men to divide his blood shed for them among themselves. But surely this is a gross and wilful perversion. If, however, say the Jews, Christ is the expected Messiah, well and good, we act up to his injunction; if not, it is a good joke to torture a poor Christian to death on pretence of obeying a precept of the author of Christianity. It is said that Sultan Mahmood strove to root out the practice; but as it was based on religion, it may be doubted whether it has so completely gone out of fashion as we should desire.

I must confess that the Jews stoutly repudiate such a notion or practice, and complain of it as one of the Greek calumnies against them. So a friend of mine who has long resided in Turkey and Egypt regards it. He says, however, that he heard of it, and further that when the matter came before the courts of the country it was disproved. Nowadays, at all events, if there is any such practice, it must be of very rare occurrence. The exceptional truth has, however, been exaggerated by popular gossip, until the kidnapping of Christian children and their slow death by the Jews has been a bugbear in the popular imagination.

I may here remark that Abyssinian superstition attributes to the Jews the power of turning to wild beasts for the purpose of sucking human blood.—Burton's *First Footsteps.*

For notices of African cannibalism consult Burton's *Equatorial Africa.* The Western tribes are free from this enormity.—Burton's *Journey in Ashang-Land.*

Yours very sincerely,

SAMBHU C. MOOKERJEE.

March 1, 1876.

My dear Rajendra,—I see that in your article in the last part enclosed herewith, you cite the same passages in the Bible relating to human sacrifice which I mentioned in my letter to you.

I forgot to mention Catlin's book on the Mandan Tribe in North America. But as you say your subject is limited to India, you need not go about hunting up all the traces of the same sanguinary barbarism in all corners of the globe. You could hardly have overlooked Ward's book which is sufficiently accurate, however bigotted and unjust to the people of India in its tone of exaggeration. Buchanan's *Researches* is also worth consulting.

Yours, &c.,

SAMBHU C. MOOKERJEE.

March 1, 10 P.M.

It occurs to me that Vambéry describes a kind of head-hunting in Central Asia. He mentions nothing religious in connection with it.

Is there anything of religious obligation in

the hereditary hate and blood feud cherished by the Bedouins, Koords, and such other tribes? Is there any religious element in the ceremony of fraternation described by Palgrave *(Hermann Agha)* and has it any connection with sacrifice?

Punditji reminds me of the belief in the Middle Ages of Jews kidnapping for burning Christian children. I wonder if the ceremony related in the *Devil in Turkey* was alluded to, or is it one of similar practices indulged in by the Jews by way of revenge for their ill usage at the hands of the Christians? Or, are both calumnies? "At a time when the Phœnician priests drenched the altars of their Moloch with the blood of their Canaanitish victims, and pitiless Druids quartered human sacrifices in the sacred groves of the early Britons, the fury of the great Hindu idol at Juggernaut was propitiated with the same spirit of fanaticism that still kindles the devotion of thousands, who prostrate themselves under his car or mutilate themselves on his shrines."—Sullivan's *Princes of India*, p. 9. Human flesh was the food of the horses of Diomed. The horses of heroes were sacrificed on their tombs.—*Ibid*, p. 536, notes.

March 21, 1876.

For a case of human sacrifice in Bengal among the *Saktas*, in 1832, see the *Asiatic Journal*, August, 1832, vol. VIII. Anand Babu says that some 20 years ago one occurred in the Kriteswari temple, Murshidabad, and that it is still in vogue very privately in Tippera.

August 19.

Human sacrifices seem to have been made at the altar of Diana Œthia.—See Euson on National Government, I., p. 49. Consult Stoddard's Study of History on the Ancient Americans, also Abbe Raynal's voluminous work.

From the Rev. Krishna Mohan Banerjee.

Ballygunge,
March 9, 1876.

My dear Friend,—I thank you cordially for

your kind letter of yesterday which reached me as I was getting into my carriage with my family going to church.

I accept as expressions of kind friendship what you have written and with the greater self-satisfaction that it comes from one who is himself a *de facto* Doctor of Literature and a profound observer and judge of men and manners. A verdict from such a quarter is in itself of greater value than the certificate of a miscellaneous body however privileged by law.

* * *

Heartily thanking you again for your affectionate expressions of kindness,

I remain, my dear friend,

Yours most sincerely,

K. M. BANERJEE.

P. S.—I shall take the chance of seeing you one day before another week is over, about 5 P.M., and confer on the subject of a lecture or of an article or both.

K. M. B.

From General Napier Campbell.

9, Russell Street,
Calcutta, September 17, 1882.

My dear Sir,—I am much obliged to you for your kindness in sending me a number of your Magazine. You are quite right in conjecturing that some of the views expressed in the article headed "A Plea for Calcutta" are regarded by me as not "irrational." I entirely agree with that portion of it which protests against the yearly exodus to Simla and points out its evil consequences. I am happy to be able to say that in this matter the course I have consistently pursued is based on your view of it.

It is always a pleasure to me to hear from any native of this country that the opinions and views I hold are such as commend themselves to the upright ones of India, and as one of them your estimation of them is noticed.

I have no doubt we should agree how I feel towards this country and its people. Yours, &c.,

NAPIER CAMPBELL.

From Mr. Meredith Townsend.

The Spectator Office,
1, Wellington Street, Strand,
London, W. C., February 21, 1883.

Dear Sir,—I am much obliged to you for forwarding "Reis and Rayyet," though I am sorry to see that, after an absence of nearly a quarter of a century, Calcutta is becoming to me only a dim recollection. I do not quite understand, I confess, why men so able as yourself should prefer to publish in a foreign tongue instead of making a literature of your own. But doubtless you have sufficient reasons.

Why do you not publish an account of your life as Minister of Tippera? It would be of great interest to Englishmen, whose difficulty is to understand how the organism of a Native State is maintained.

Yours truly,
MEREDITH TOWNSEND.

To Mr. Meredith Townsend.

My dear Sir,—So long ago as February 1883, in

acknowledging receipt of the weekly *Reis and Rayyet*, you wrote to me expressing your surprise why we Indians should prefer to publish in a foreign tongue instead of making a literature of our own. In the end, however, you say—"But doubtless you have sufficient reasons."

And so we have. We might have created one of the finest literatures in the world, without making any impression in the camp of our British rulers and, of course, without advancing our political or even social status. Nay, the truth is that we have created a literature, and a very respectable literature it is. You who were a Bengali scholar in your time in India, having conducted a Bengali weekly, I believe, for a couple of years (in regard to which and indeed your early life in India generally I may remark, in passing, I should like to have your particular recollections), you would be astonished at the present state of our language —its copiousness in terms of all kinds and its wealth of literature. All that copiousness and all that wealth have not helped us one whit, or rescued us from our degradation. Hence we are compelled to journalism and authorship in a foreign tongue—to make English a kind of second vernacular to us, if possible. You have no idea of the enormous personal sacrifice involved in this.

English does not offer us an earnest of future. It is those that cultivate Bengali who will be remembered hereafter by their countrymen, as they are most read now. But we who write in English have to make this sacrifice for the Fatherland.

You concluded with a suggestion—"Why do you not publish an account of your life as Minister of Tippera?" The answer is—because I might then compromise my master and the little State I served. And, secondly, because I might thereby close the only career open to me in Native India. British officials try their utmost to keep able and writing natives out of the Native States, and any indiscretion on my part would arm them with a deadly weapon against me and the small class of aspiring natives educated in Western learning who can manage States.

However, I have done the next best thing —published a small volume of "Travels through Bengal to Tippera," giving glimpses of life in a Native State, and it now awaits an adequate review from your pen.

Yours truly,

SAMBHU C. MOOKERJEE.

Mookerjee made the acquaintance of Sir Howard Russell, the king of war correspondents, during H. R. H. the Prince of Wales' visit in the cold weather of 1875-76. Sir Howard, it will be remembered, was a prominent member of the Prince's suite throughout that memorable excursion, and afterwards became its chronicler. In a note from the royal camp he writes "I hope to be able, ere I leave India, and indeed after I have done so, to improve our acquaintance by letter." His anticipation was realized, as the following letter will show :—

From Dr. W. H. Russell.

"La Piccola Sentinella,"

Ischera, June 23, 1883.

My dear Sir,—Your letter of the 17th April last, after as many unconscious wanderings as Ulysses and far more extensive scope of travel, came here to me at last, and here your answer, if sent by return post, will find me, I fear: for I am trying the virtues of these world-renowned waters in the cure of *anno domini* rheumatism and some of the other ills that flesh is heir to. It would give me sincere regret if my silence could have led you to suppose I neglected your communication wilfully. I went to Egypt this time twelvemonth as an amateur, for I was not allowed to be a professional, and I only returned from the scene of very interesting events a short time ago, laid up with fever and debility. If "Reis and Rayyet" is sent to my office I will have it forwarded, and I shall accede with pleasure to your request for an exchange with the "Army and Navy Gazette." My small experience of India has led me to take a profound interest in the country and its people and to appreciate the capacity of such men as Salar Jung and Madhava Rao in the highest work of government; but I am sorry to say our general knowledge of the greatest empire ever given to an alien race to rule for good has not been warmed by the breath of sympathy, without which the finest administrative talents are as hollow brass and tinkling cymbals. As I wrote in 1858-59, "If England loses India it will be from want of sympathy with its people." I am not sufficiently versed in the merits of the controversy over the Ilbert Bill which has caused so much heat to express an opinion, but I confess I have so much faith in Lord Ripon's sense of justice that I would be inclined *primâ facie* to support any measure he favoured, even if all the dogs of war in the Mofussil and all the powers of opiumdom and indigodom were ranged against it. * * *

So far there are perils in advance and in retreat, and perhaps it would have been the safest course if the Government had waited a little longer till some good case appeared for the reform or extension of the jurisdiction of native Magistrates.

I intend to get back to England, and indeed I was looking for a seat in Parliament. I need not say, without any ambition to do more than make my experience useful, for I have no personal aims to serve ; but the luxury of a seat is too costly, and besides I am an impossible politician, for I am a Tory and yet a Liberal. I believe in a loyal and conservative attachment to the monarchy and the fullest exercise of all the best powers of a Republic, and I have a fervent faith in the force which Justice gives a State and the repose and security which can and must be enjoyed by every Empire whose rulers obey the command —"Be just and fear not."

I am, my dear Sir,
Yours truly,
W. H. RUSSELL.

From Major Evans Bell.

110. Holland Road,
Kensington, W., London, July 27, 1883.

Dear Sir,—You will see by the copy of the *Times* giving an account of our proceedings of the 23rd instant, that the Liberal friends of India here have not been idle in supporting the recent policy of Lord Ripon, and the ticket I enclose will remind you of the next step that is about to be taken. But of course the most important piece of news by this mail—which you will have received by telegrams many hours before I can post this letter—is the satisfactory reception and reply given by Lord Kimberley to the deputation from Sir Alexander Arbuthnot's Anglo-Indian Committee. But neither we nor you must relax our efforts till all danger is past of any serious modification of the Bill. You probably know something of the labour and anxiety and endless details in getting up a successful public meeting—but you can have little notion of what it is in this great world of London. Do not you, or any Indian, fail to remember that nearly all the credit of our work here at this crisis is due to Mr. Hodgson Pratt, whose noble exertions on behalf of every good cause can never be too highly appreciated. I have wrapped up in the *Times* one of the 500 bills drawn up by Mr. Pratt and widely circulated among the working men's clubs, of which there are more than 80 in London. Of the small handbills, one of which I enclose, 10,000 have been distributed. The Anglo-Indian Committee cannot venture to hold a real public meeting. The Radical artizans would spoil any such meeting by their voices and votes.

Believe me, very truly yours,

EVANS BELL.

From Major Evans Bell.

Boston, United States of America,
December 24, 1883.

My dear Sir,—I received your letter of the 23rd of September at New York, U. S., more than a month ago, but have been so constantly on the move, seeing as much as can be seen, and doing as much as can be done, in a brief tour of two months, in this great and wonderful country, (larger than all Europe, and peopled by 55 millions of the Anglo-Saxon race) that I have never had time to answer it. If Mr. Knight, as I doubt not he will, publishes in the *Statesman* a short abstract of the lectures on the British Empire in India that I have been delivering here, it will give you some notion of what I mean when I say that I have been endeavouring to take a new departure in Indian politics, and to suggest to the foremost men of India the principles on which their claims to enfranchisement should be made to rest, and from which they should not tolerate any with-

drawal or diminution. * * *
But I think I can do better work in London, having struck the keynote that I wanted. It is clear now that the opponents of the Ilbert Bill have so far succeeded as to keep up the unconstitutional and anarchical distinction between the Indian and the European citizen, or rather the Indian subject and European citizen. At this main point we in England ought to hammer away day after day, exposing, denouncing and ridiculing it from every point of view, answering each objection as it arises.

But this can never be done until the true champions of a British Empire have an organ of their own. The work must be done or it will not be done at all, in London. Men like Col. Osborn and * * have every qualification but funds. We are at the great crisis now, and the opportunity will soon pass away.

Believe me, sincerely yours,

EVANS BELL.

To Mr. G. Vencataramaniah.

Editor of the "Indian Leisure Hour,"

Vizianagram.

Reis and Rayyet Office,

August 14, 1883.

Dear Sir,—I duly received your note of the 20th ultimo and the pages of "The Indian Leisure Hour" accompanying.

Sárangadhara is, indeed, a most promising production, and I have resolved to give it the widest publicity in our paper. You will, I trust, excuse me for withholding the fact of its original publication. It is my practice to acknowledge the source from which I derive anything, however trifling. There are journals which habitually pilfer ideas and news and even whole paragraphs and articles from *Reis and Rayyet* without acknowledgment. To these too I give their due whenever I borrow from them, though of late, at the instance of friends, I am, by way of reprisal, adopting a system of admitting quotations without naming the source. I make this statement because it goes against my grain to print the poem as if it was our own. But I do this on purpose, and in the interest of the poem itself. People do not care for a piece that has appeared before. Few would look into even a little known work of a great poet, if published in a newspaper. "Oh! they have filled their columns with a long extract," or "It is old chaff," they say. When the source from which a piece is derived happens to be obscure, the chance of anybody attending to it is still less. A fortnightly publication of a distant district of the Benighted Presidency can hardly hope to command an audience of the general public. When that journal is a native affair, the thing is out of the question. It is an unhappy prejudice, no doubt, but there is no help for it. Appearing from time to time, in fragments, in "The Indian Leisure Hour," the poem may be said to have received no publication as yet. I wished to give it every advantage and have accordingly published it as if it were our own. My object, indeed, is twofold. I wish to encourage the young author by bringing out his work under the most favourable circumstances. The appearance of a poem in a high class journal of literature as well as politics is no ordinary recommendation ; it is tantamount to an appreciative criticism. In the next place, I mean to test the literary calibre of our public. We have got, I suspect, few true judges of high literature. Poetry is still less understood, I fear. It will be interesting to watch the reception of this essay in English verse by a native of India. Hereafter, there will be time enough to surprise the public with the origin of the work. Meanwhile, please communicate this letter to your young friend. His poem has many defects to be sure, but there is stuff in him. Let him go on and prosper. I need scarcely say that I long to know his name and all particulars about him, his birth, his education and pursuits. Yours, &c.,

SAMBHU C. MOOKERJEE.

To Mr. G. Venkata Appa Rao.

September 17, 1883.

My dear Mr. Venkata Appa Rao,— I duly received your two letters of the 29th August and 4th September current. I am glad that you have taken the trouble to write so fully. I take a great interest in the career of a young poet like you and the accounts of your life are most welcome. The discouragements you have experienced are nothing extraordinary; every writer of genius or any originality, certainly every poet, must reckon upon them. Still less reason is there to wonder at your travail. The number of men that understand good literature is small in every land. Those that understand poetry are still fewer. Look at the fate of poets in Europe! In India, the case is desperate. The Anglo-Indians, though educated, are not a learned or critical class. What shall we say of the natives? A native writer is under a peculiar disadvantage. The natives generally wait upon the European judgment. Even the knowing ones are too prudent to risk their opinion. The Europeans are apt to regard a native's attempt to court the Muses in a European tongue as almost an impertinence, rather than an act of rashness, which, no doubt, it is. The spectacle of a black fellow, not content with writing prose, going so far as to dabble in metre, is apt to deprive them of the legitimate exercise of reason. Then the modern blank verse that you attempt in *Sárangadhara* is far from popular, I suspect. The jingling rhymes of Pope still occupy the minds of men and pass for true poetry. But never mind. Don't be discouraged. You have parts. Improve them by cultivation. Read and reflect. Read not poetry only, but all kinds of books. Above all, observe. Observe man and nature and their works. Travel, if you get an opportunity. If not, make the most of your immediate neighbourhood. Go into the remote villages, the woods, the hills; go to the sea-shore; watch the sun and the moon; watch clouds and storms; watch sunbeams and the dew; watch the stars of Heaven and the thunder and lightning and the waves of old ocean. Watch waterfalls and the running brooks. Nor forget to notice the beautiful and the uncomely in the human form divine. And, last not least, follow the operations of the heart, your own and others'; measure their strength as well as weakness. Remember what others have remarked on these things, but never depend upon others. Trust your ownself, give tether to your own powers. You must read a good deal, but inasmuch as you write in a tongue not your own, you must master the language. Read carefully, to see how those to the manner born express themselves. At first you must imitate others until you acquire command sufficiently to chalk out, if possible, a new path suiting your genius. If you write from true inspiration, when full of your subject, you cannot fail to succeed. More hereafter.

Yes, do give us a satire on the present controversy by way of a relaxation.

Yours most truly,
SAMBHU C. MOOKERJEE.

To Mr. Venkata Appa Rao.

December 28, 1884.

My dear Appa Rao,—I have just returned from Tippera and so read your affectionate enclosure to the business* communication addressed to me as Editor. And as I have plenty of leisure I had better answer it at once, though I have no other paper to write upon but this crumpled sheet of the Business Department. Anything to show regard and affection, if the feeling be real ! And for ourselves, we descendants of gymnosophists are used* to inscribe our thoughts on palm and plantain leaves and bark.

* In the first instance the words were "official" and "accustomed." They were then altered to "business" and "used." Reference is made to these alterations a few lines lower down.

Your letter does not require prompt attention, but as you look up to me for advice, there is always a reason for writing whenever I can afford the time: the disposition is always present. Nor need I be in want of materials. I may chat with you on paper when in the mood, with perhaps some little advantage to yourself. Suppose, for instance, I criticise my own writing—this very letter. I may tell you, what might interest you to know, that I have penned through the word "accustomed" not because it is any way wrong or inaccurate or infelicitous, but because I wished to show that a simpler word would do, and be perhaps more expressive because it is downright English, which the other is not. You must be aware of this. One who has read so much of the best poetry in the language, specially of the unsophisticated earlier period, one, indeed, who is a poet into the bargain, cannot but be familiar with the first principles of a pure, idiomatic, nervous diction. But I wished to present another example to youth, which is naturally fascinated by the music of voluminous words and of rolling periods, in order to give it confidence in its knowledge and taste. You see I have been breaking the rule myself in the last sentence, but then the rule has its exception—in fact, there are more rules on the subject than one. The Latin part of the language is not to be despised. There can be no rhythm, generally speaking, no wide sweep of sound, without its help.

Again for " official," I substitute " business " as the right word in the opening sentence. " Official " would have done equally, or better perhaps, in the way of literary expression. But I was afraid you might, on my authority, describe such a letter as yours to the editor by the same word in a matter-of-fact business way. In that way it is a " business letter." To call it " official " is to speak of it in a rather ormal way.

Thus you see I have come to the end of my

space! I am glad to see your list of reading. It is comprehensive and very creditable to your years. At another time I shall make some remarks on the subject. Just now I must hasten to dinner which is announced.

I am obliged to you for your kind wish that my evening may be happy and tranquil. I can scarcely hope so. I have a great capacity for enjoyment and a disposition to tranquility. But those who have a strong sense of duty and desire to live for their country and the world, in however obscure a sphere or way, must be prepared for misery. But I am called again and must close with my most affectionate regards.

Yours,

SAMBHU C. MOOKERJEE.

To Mr. G. Venkata Appa Rao.

January 27, 1884.

My dear Bard,—I duly received your several letters and must apologise for my long silence. The fact is, I have been very busy and besides knew you would be so too, between prose and poetry, examination and recreation. Even now I do not intend to disturb you in the midst of your serious occupations with a long letter. But it is time enough to send you an assurance that your correspondent lives. How long do you stay at Madras? Let me hear all about your examination and society there. Who are the leading men as regards letters and politics and position? Who are your best public speakers? I should like to hear also of the social and political movements. What are the prospects of widow marriage? I see that native society was divided on the subject of the party to Mr. Carmichael. What is the opinion on the subject now? Are the influential gentlemen who honoured the retiring member of the Government ashamed of themselves or the worse thought of by the public? Are the promoters of the counter-demonstration admired for their courage? Have they been in bad odour with the Europeans since? What do they say of poor Mr. Wallace? But I fear that, like Napoleon the Great, I am too much given to asking questions. You may answer at leisure, or not at all.

Vizianagram has come with a heap of camp-followers. I expected a visit from the brightest of the nine gems of his *sabha*, but you have not yet turned up. So I conclude you are hard at work at Madras.

* * *

Yours sincerely,
SAMBHU C. MOOKERJEE.

From Major Evans Bell.

110, Holland Road,
London, W., Feb. 8, 1884.

My dear Sir,—By this time I calculate that a brief abstract of the lectures I lately delivered in the United States of America may have been published in the Calcutta "Statesman," and, I should hope, would have received some attention from you. Unless I am very much mistaken, I have in these lectures taken a new departure and set forth an intelligible principle, which all educated Indians,—if there is any political instinct stirring among them,—should adopt as their central idea and animating doctrine in every appeal and effort for their emancipation from the usurped supremacy of European birth and blood. That pretended supremacy—very real, by the bye, in many aspects—has no true warrant in international law or in the municipal law of Great Britain. I regard it as utterly incompatible with Imperial stability and with sincere allegiance. You should set before yourselves the watchword "British subject, British citizen," and though you may accept concessions and instalments, never profess to be content with anything less than the full recognition of that Imperial axiom. At present you really have not the full rights of an Indian citizen in India. You must assert yourselves boldly and firmly, but without bitterness. You will do nothing against European pride, prejudice, and class interests without a distinct ideal and irreducible demand. I could carry on a grand campaign here on these lines—but my campaign, I fear, is over. I had never resources or materials for such a fight against principalities and powers, and I am now fairly beaten and do not expect to live in London much longer.

Believe me,

Sincerely yours,

EVANS BELL.

Sir William Hunter has suffered severely at the hands of literary pirates. There is a large class of men, who, without a vestige of original power and destitute even of the minor gift of plodding industry, are always prepared to pick the brains of a successful author. Sir William's *Brief History of India* had been hashed up for service as a schoolbook by one of these professional pilferers. His just anger, as well as his high sense of the dignity of letters, are fully expressed in the next letter.

From Mr. W. W. Hunter.

Middleton Street,
Calcutta, February 29, 1884.

My dear Sir,—I am obliged for your little paragraph about the piratical abridgment of my Brief History, and I shall look forward with interest to the further remarks which you promise. I believe it is to the true interest of the Indian Press to denounce such action on the part of the book-maker, for nothing reflects deeper or more widespread disgrace on the literature of a country than such practices. Men of letters in India must be careful of the growing reputation of the literary profession and of the literary class. I have too slight an interest in the book itself to take notice of the ignoble felonies upon it, but I think you are rendering service to Indian literature by protesting against them.

I am,
Very faithfully yours,
W. W. HUNTER.

From Major Evans Bell.

110, Holland Road,
London, W., Feb. 29, 1884.

Dear Sir,—I have written to you more than once urging you to adopt as your political *minimum* and *ultimatum* the principle of "British subject, British citizen." That definite and intelligible demand forms a sufficient centre for the whole programme of political emancipation. You may have seen in the *Statesman* during January and February (February 3rd is the last I have received) some assertions of this principle. These are all of my writing—though sometimes Mr. Knight takes a few of my sentences and frames them in one of his own articles. It is on this line that the battle must be fought, and the line of battle is not as yet half developed. And although you can not be too active and stirring on your own ground, I think you understand almost as well as I do that real progress towards victory can only be made here—in

London. I will add that it can only be made through the Radical party, which is rapidly becoming the strongest element in Liberal politics. Take to mind what I wrote to you regarding a paper to be managed by Col. Osborn and * * . In them you have a force that ought not to be wasted or turned in other directions.

* * *

Believe me, truly yours,

EVANS BELL.

To Mr. G. Venkata Appa Rao.

Calcutta, May 20, 1884.

My dear young Bard,—You see, I find no difficulty in addressing you—that is, since I have had the happiness of knowing you. Before that I must have experienced some difficulty. In point of fact you obviated it by your first copious communication giving an account of yourself. I always find myself in a fix in writing to a stranger, especially an Oriental, for the first time.

June 3.

There ! There you may read my defence for my long silence, including my seeming neglect of your affectionate despatch of the 2nd May ! There you may see how unjust is your natural suspicion that I do not reciprocate your feelings ! After weeks of ineffectual wishing, I at last sat down on the 20th to give you a reply, determined to finish my epistle at that sitting, but lo ! before I had fairly plunged into the introduction I was peremptorily interrupted, and the scarcely begun note was lost in the mass of unfinished MSS. on an editor's table. I have today lighted upon it and shall try to add to it a few sentences, if I cannot finish it.

I was saying that I never experienced any difficulty in addressing Europeans, because I knew their customs ; and whether I approved of them or not, it was sufficient that they were their own. I had only to write to them as they would write among themselves, and this I could do without compunction. Not so with our Indian brethren. Here the ground is wholly uncertain. We are not sure what will be acceptable—the idea varies with individuals. * * The reason lies on the surface. We are Orientals, employing an Western tongue. * * Just as we easily lapse into our vernacular idiotisms in our conversation and writing, so we are addicted to Indian forms of address and superscription in our correspondence. Perhaps, we all have a sneaking preference for our own. Nationality is hard to suppress. Oriental languages are rich in etiquette of all kinds. On the contrary, the English has far too few forms of epistolary address. Its barrenness is not calculated to satisfy us. What wonder then, that we should show, even in English correspondence, a tendency to differentiate varieties of station and feeling? For instance, my Brahmanic aristocracy revolts at the idea of *Sir*-ing a Sudra. *Sir* is translated in Bengali or Sanscrit *Mahásaya*—a common enough term of address among us, but, strictly speaking, one to be given to Brahmans only. This speciality of the word has been almost lost under the influence of our modern system of education in British India and in the progress of democratic ideas of equality, but it was very well understood in the past. Now-a-days we *mahásaya* each other and everybody of respectable appearance and dress. There is no distinction between Brahmans and Sudras in the forms of speech or spoken language. Formerly few would think of saying *mahásaya* to a non-Brahman. The Brahman who used such an address towards the Sudra would be regarded as either very ignorant or very servile. Good Sudras would themselves be shocked at being so addressed by the chief of the twice-born. About the use of *Sir*—the English equivalent of *Mahásaya*—there is still less difficulty, if possible. The etiquette that differentiates class from class is confined to vernacular correspondence. In Bengali the epistolary forms reserved for Brahmans would never be employed towards other castes. But there is no such distinction in English. We indiscriminately bandy terms of respect between ourselves. In English we are all equal. I, perhaps, am the sole representative of old world compunction—the one remnant of the dark ages lingering yet in a time of enlightenment. For I am about the sole repository of the knowledge and the feelings of the past, and I cling to time-honoured traditions with a sentimental attachment. It goes against my grain to subscribe myself Obedient Servant to any Hindu, and I generally avoid *sir*-ing non-Brahmans.

June 22.

Not that I have been always so minded in my younger days. When I was at college and for some years after, I was radical and democratic, but the phase passed away, and latterly I think I have come to a truer estimate of things, appreciating differences and submitting to nature. But you should not run away with the notion that I am unduly vain of my caste, looking down upon others, &c., &c. I know no illiberality. I have always been a seeker for truth and an asserter of justice in everything. My language, I know, deceives. I scold and ridicule. It is hard to suppress the workings of a vivacious fancy. But I never really despise. As I rigidly exact from my own consciousness justice to others, I have schooled myself to contemn no man,—nay, no thing. I am disposed to see the fitness of all things. My argument to my Ahriman is—If the Lord Almighty can permit a being or thing exist, why should not I, who cannot conquer my own head-aches? That does not dispose of the matter entirely, in all its aspects, but the thought is well calculated to subdue pride and conceit, to bring us down to our proper level, to open our eyes to the fitness of things. It has certainly been of the highest use to me in my struggle, within myself, with passion. I recommend it to all who seek me or listen to me in earnest. My dear young Brahman, the son of Bharadwaja (I need not tell you that it is myself) could not send you from the banks of the Bhagirathi, in famed Aryavarta, a *mantra* more precious. Sir Walter Scott, notwithstanding the library he had written, conceived that he had something left to say before he left the world, and he said it to his dear son-in-law—"Be a good man, John." Easier said than done, might Lockhart reply. The difficulty is about the way. The Rishis, ancient and modern, are usually silent. The consideration I have mentioned will, I venture to think, be found as successful as any other. I see I have digressed; but I will not, having regard to the importance of the matter, apologise. Apart from that, the complaint against digression is not legitimate in this behalf. Digression is the very soul of epistolary correspondence. Friendly letters, to my mind, ought not to be stately narratives, or rigidly construed statements, or elaborate arguments.

They should be of the nature of familiar intercourse. For my part, I love to talk with you through the post, giving myself up to the bent of the hour or the suggestion of the moment, the more so as I cannot hope to see you within any reasonable period.

Here I had better close. I began on the 20th May and this is the 22nd June—more than a month to write a single letter ! What are you about ? Did you commence the political poem you contemplated ? Try your hand at ballads and stanzas in different metres. Your versification is defective. Only constant practice can give you an easy, smooth, bounding pen. * * Vale !

SAMBHU C. MOOKERJEE.

From Professor H. M'Neil.

123, Turk Street,
San Francisco, Dec. 5, 1884.

Dear Doctor,—Permit me to introduce myself to you. I am Professor of *Materia Medica* in the Hahnemann Medical College of San

Francisco. I am now engaged in collecting the characteristics of the homœopathic Materia Medica for publication. Having read your letter to the American Institute of Homœopathy dated April 1873 and seeing how much valuable material you are able to contribute to such a work, I make bold to ask you to either inform me where I can find such if published, or if not published, if you would be so kind as to furnish me with as many of the characteristics as you can conveniently furnish to me. When the work is published, you will receive credit for every symptom incorporated in the work.

Very respectfully,

H. M'Neil.

From Major Evans Bell.

National Liberal Club,
London, June 25, 1885.

Dear Sir,—I really forget whether, when I forwarded you a copy of my *Memoir of General Briggs*, I accompanied it by a letter or not. I have been for several months in such a distracted and confused state, owing partly to illness, partly to troubles which contributed to bring on that illness, that I have lost count of time and circumstances. I know I wrote briefly to you a short time before the publication, because a very kind paragraph in *Reis and Rayyet* reminded me of the fact. The illness and untoward events above referred to both delayed and curtailed the last chapter of the book, which I had intended to be much longer, and had hoped to make of some importance. The present political crisis here forms a most valuable opportunity for Indian reformers at the centre of Imperial affairs—of whom there are so few—if they were only able to take advantage of it. I am, as you know, a Radical myself, but I recognise the value of the occasional advent of Conservatives to power, so far as it brings younger and fresher minds to the exercise of executive power and opens to them the arena and the archives of our bureaucratic system. It was owing to an accidental and temporary conjuncture of that nature, very much like the present one, that we saved the State of Mysore from annexation in 1867. Lord Randolph Churchill has comparative youth, freedom from departmental attachments, and great courage, with a burning desire to distinguish himself during the few months of authority that he will enjoy (for you may rely on it the Tories will be swept away at the General Eelection). Under the strange disadvantages of my actual situation, I shall endeavour to make some impression on him. He seems to have acquired some ideas of a healthy tendency during his flying tour through India.

I want to see your Associations directing their attention and their efforts at certain great principles—what we call *fighting to points and sticking to them.* One of these I have briefly formulated in the last page but one of "Briggs"—"Union but not Uniformity." This strikes at once at annexation and at over-legislation. "Perfect citizenship for every British subject"—that is another, directed against race distinctions, very imperfectly broken down as yet—for the Ilbert Bill, as modified, was a trifle,—and which constitute political slavery.

All these points, and the financial question, though calling for every species of activity in India, cannot be so well fought out there as in London. I feel I could do much in the five or ten years of active life that may be left to me, but I feel that my resources are at an end. Twenty years of struggle against the Indian Civil Service—the real enemy—have beaten me at last. I see that progress has been made, and that this is the time for redoubling our blows, but I shall have no part in the victory, should it come in our days. I am at present in every sense beaten out of the field, for I have no house in London—or elsewhere—and my only address is as above.

I know how the brief period of Conservative power *should* be utilized here, and I trust that in India you will not allow the occasion to pass away without some decided movement.

Believe me, sincerely yours,

EVANS BELL.

The following letter is short, but it brings many of the Doctor's characteristics into strong relief. The "despatch" was an article in *Reis and Rayyet.* He never failed to show gratitude for the slightest services. The "old gentleman" is Raja Rajendralala Mitra, who practically edited the *Hindoo Patriot* after the death of Babu Kristodas Pal. Mookerjee had marked with sorrow the deterioration of the paper towards the success of which he had largely contributed.

The "Brahman neighbour" was a resident of Sibpur of small means, who had been driven by the Howrah Municipality to obtain redress in the civil court. Mookerjee felt for the old Brahman as for a relative; and the story of his sufferings was afterwards told in the columns of *Reis and Rayyet* in a trenchant attack on local bumbledom. Mookerjee's reverence for age was sincere and deep. The "old gentleman" in the last sentence was his correspondent's father, whom Mookerjee admired as a brilliant conversationalist and a man of very liberal views.

The postscript refers to "Ram Sharma" or "Ram," the poet of *Mookerjee's Magazine* and *Reis and Rayyet.*

To Babu Kisari Mohan Ganguli.

July 2, 1885.

My dear Kisari,—Thanks for your despatch. I am glad you are getting on tolerably well with the old gentleman. I hope he will appreciate you unselfishly enough to provide you suitably and honourably on the *Patriot,* which badly wants looking after, especially after the depths to which it was brought down on the death of poor Kristodas.

Why don't you do the thing for your

Brahman neighbour? I have no time, I assure you, to go through the papers.

How is the old gentleman? My *pronams* to him.

Yours affectionately,

SAMBHU C. MOOKERJEE.

P. S.—By the bye, Ram Babu is made miserable by the Public Library *takeeds* (reminders) for the copy of the *Gita* he got for you from there. Do send it back, now you have done reviewing it.

S. C. M.

The next letter will speak for itself. It is full of interest, relating as it does to the policy which Mookerjee consistently endeavoured to adopt in the conduct of *R. & R.* The great fault of Calcutta journals is their note of provinciality. They cannot be read at Madras or Bombay, Lahore or even at Allahabad with any interest. As an experienced editor, whose ideal was a lofty one, Mookerjee always sought to prevent his contributors from taking up subjects of purely local interest. His control over them was as close and searching as a Roman centurion's over his valiant infantry.

The Anglo-Indian *Poison Tree* was an unauthorised translation of Babu Bunkim Chander Chatterji's *Bisha Vriksha* which saw the light about this time.

The concluding sentences will show how strict Mookerjee was in speaking of qualifications in a certificate or testimonial. He used to say that a great responsibility attached to persons giving characters to others. It is much to be lamented that this responsibility sits very lightly on the shoulders of many people. Nothing is more common than the use of superlatives in praising a person recommended to others for employment.

To Babu Kisari Mohan Ganguli.

Reis and Rayyet Office,
Calcutta, August 21, 1885.

My dear Kisari,—I have not read the article on Nundalal Chatterji you allude to. The fact is, I am averse to making the paper a vehicle of local and personal grievances. We have already sinned enough in that line and it is time to retrieve our character. It is this provinciality or localism that has, notwithstanding our brilliant conduct, been in the way of the general popularity of the journal, specially in the more distant parts of the Empire. Now that enquiries are being made from Madras and Bombay and attention is being drawn to it even in England, it is time to make *R. & R.*, what it professes to be, an imperial organ of the most advanced Indian thought and culture. Sibpur and other places "over the water" have too much engrossed us. The case to which you refer has already been noticed in the Press, I believe, as much as could be reasonably desired. So let us employ our space and energies to better purpose.

Yes, you may damn the English or rather Anglo-Indian "Poison Tree" to your heart's content, and you will be in good company.

There are heaps of books and pamphlets to notice. Next week I will send you a quantity.

I attended to your application dutifully and will not lose sight of it when the time comes. I sent it through Satis to the Honorary Secretary, although Jogesh was right when he told you that it was not on the clerk's list. But there is no fear of its miscarriage. I have given you an elaborate character, which I dare say will console you somewhat as coming from one who, with some powers of discrimination, will never stoop to say what is not. I hope the Union will have the luck to secure you. There would be little cause for misgiving, were it not for our Brahmanical luck.

I am sorry for the last paragraph in your note. You should not be so sensitive after having seen so much of the world. You will only be miserable if you carry this feminine shrinking with you all through life. Why can't you brave the minor ills like a man? And, after all, many of these may be mere mares' nests of your own discovery. For really I have no idea of what you refer to.

Yours affectionately,

SAMBHU C. MOOKERJEE.

The case alluded to in the next letter was one which made a considerable sensation at the time : but is now, happily, forgotten. Mr. R. Knight, editor of the *Statesman*, was prosecuted for libel by a European official attached to the service of the Maharaja of Burdwan. I was able to tender my mediation and induce Mr. Knight to make an apology for charges which, inspired as they were by good faith and a love of justice, were none the less entirely wanting in solid foundation.

From Mr. Robert Knight.

The *Statesman*,

3, Chowringhee,

Calcutta, Sept. 6, 1886.

Dear Mookerjee,—* * * I am most glad to see that you are so dexterously eliciting good out of evil in the case. It is (as you say) most difficult and invidious work, but your natural gift of humour fits you for the task in a very striking way. If *I* had but your sense of humour, I should have accomplished what—without it—I have given up all hope of doing.

Yours,
Very sincerely,
R. KNIGHT.

From Mr. Robert Knight.

The *Statesman*,
3, Chowringhee,
Calcutta, August 30, 1886.

My dear Mookerjee,—I delayed replying to your note until I knew the result of this morning's appearance. The case is postponed to December, when the Chief Justice will try it, if it comes to trial at all.

Your articles have been admirable and they are a reflection upon the whole English Press. What becomes of the freedom of the Press, if every charge made against Government servants is to be answered by a *criminal* prosecution ?

I have refrained from saying more than I felt we had a full right to say. My sub. was stupid enough to reproduce that *Delhi Gazette* article, in spite of my "orders" to produce nothing on the subject.

I want much to talk with you. * * *Reis and Rayyet* is always brilliant, and I look out for it impatiently every Sunday.

Yours most sincerely,

R. KNIGHT.

The following is a very characteristic epistle. Mookerjee's anxiety for the health of his friends was genuine. The causes of his own breakdown are also indicated here. The multiplicity of his avocations and the habitual sacrifice of his own interests to friends' seriously interfered with work and told on his health. Few among those who had the honour of knowing him were aware how thoroughly unselfish he was. Even when his whole attention should have been focussed on his paper, he shrank from giving a hint to friends not to take up his time. One result was that he was oblig- ed, almost throughout life, to work at night and could rarely retire to rest before two or three in the morning.

The fear of " Sir George " induced him to go to the Town Hall " most rashly." There we have the man! Babu Kally Prasanno Dey of the *National Magazine* is known among his friends by that nickname. Dr. Mookerjee having made an appointment with him to go to the Gibbs' memorial meeting of which Babu Kally Prasanno was the chief promoter, he could not think of backing out at the eleventh hour.

Many of his friends will read this letter with feelings of unavailing sorrow at the sacrifices which he made in order to receive their calls.

To Babu Kisari Mohan Ganguli.

January 3, 1886.

My dear Kisari,—I have been enquiring in the

office about you latterly, as it seemed an age since I had heard of you, and I felt apprehensions of sickness, unless you had gone away on some enterprise. But I could get no information. Had old Sadasiva not gone home I would have known what it was. Your paper was going to Sibpur and all was thought to be well.

Unfortunately, Pratap was away, or else I might have learnt from him. Under the circumstances, I wished a man sent to enquire. I feel a kind of presentiment of illness being the cause of your long mysterious silence. The day that the man was to go or the day previous I learnt that you had been to Janai and been long detained there, and had at length escaped to Sibpur with life and limb of self and family. I had myself been suffering from the last *Bijayá*, off and on, for the greater part of the time. I could not take the change that I had intended and which had become so necessary for my health. I was not even able to take a peep into the flooded districts. I intended to surprise you on one of my days of tolerable health, but the obligation to give audience to numbers of people swallows up all available time and even hours for meals and sleep, and then the latter end of the week with its responsibilities comes upon me.

I am suffering today, though I went out most rashly for an hour to the Town Hall for fear of Sir George. On Friday night I thought I had an attack of cholera. I was certainly in an agony and am still prostrate in the whole system.

Yours affectionately,

SAMBHU C. MOOKERJEE.

From Major Evans Bell.

National Liberal Club,
Trafalgar Square,
London, October 1, 1886.

My dear Sir,— * * *

Your kind recollections and appreciation of

what I have done, or endeavoured to do, in the advocacy of a truly Imperial policy for India, are even more encouraging and refreshing to me than the material help you have placed in my way. Although there have been some hopeful signs of late of attention being roused, and of able men in public positions, strong and independent in their own private resources—the great essential—being drawn towards Indian affairs, the few of us who have worked at them for years, do not, on the whole, meet with much encouragement. The only effectual plan for keeping the subject alive, and for keeping influential men up to the mark, is that of "pegging away" at them at every favourable occasion with that special knowledge and that sound doctrine—easily recognizable by the Liberal mind—which so few writers or publicists of any sort in London possess. My ideal machinery for *transforming*,—for more than *reform* is wanted—the Government of India, is, as I have said before, a weekly paper under the control of Colonel Osborn and * *, not exclusively or even specially devoted to Indian topics, but always on the watch and ready for the attack. The Civil Service is the enemy, and the objective point in almost every advance towards a better policy. The chief principles we want to establish as accepted principles of the Liberal party are, in my opinion,

I. British subject, British citizen—no distinction to be recognized in law.

II. A constitution truly Imperial,—federal with reference to the Indian Principalities, on their conforming to certain conditions defining the princely prerogative and limiting princely expenditure—partially representative in British Provinces, with the right of interpellation in open Council.

The ultimate goal should be "the United States of India."

I think you are quite right—singularly prescient and judicious,—both as to the volunteering question, and as to the recent suggestion of an Indian being appointed Legal Member of Council. I need not repeat your arguments. The doctrine should be, no rule of exclusion and the most eligible man to be chosen. There is another more difficult and debatable point, on which I do not for the moment recollect your declared views—whether there should be a lower scale of salary for the same appointment when a Native occupies it instead of an Englishman. I think decidedly you should not only tolerate but uphold such a distinction. There is no violation of principle in it whatever. The person whose domicile is in India may well be adequately compensated by a smaller salary than that calculated to attract a man from Europe. (I say nothing here of the absolute extravagance of some salaries; that will not weaken but strengthen our case). We are then enabled to insist, in addition to the political and Imperial arguments on the economical advantages—necessities, there soon may be—of replacing Europeans in office by Indians. In the case of seats on the High Court Bench alone, I feel some little aversion to having two scales of salary, but I would even give way there, as a matter of policy and without, as I contend, any sacrifice of principle, in the case of Judges having their domicile in India.

But you are quite right as to the particular case of the Legal Member of Council. It is obvious that the Viceroy and his colleagues must have a legal adviser in whose perfect sympathy with British interests they can have implicit confidence, and with whom they can confer with absolute openness and intimate unreserve in any great crisis. It is owing to the anomalous and unnatural conditions of British power in India that no Indian could, at present at least, stand in those relations to the Viceroy, but so it is, and it must be recognized as a fact. I think there ought to be, and that there well could be, at least one Indian member of the Executive, but the Legal Member must be an Englishman, and must often confer with the Viceroy apart and in secret.

I do not know whether you noticed my remarks in the *Statesman*, inserted by Mr. Knight as from a correspondent, on the subject of Naoroji's and Ghose's late candidature. I did not *intend* them for publication, though I told Mr. Knight he could print their substance if he liked. I said to him that I was afraid the candidates would never forgive me, if they knew my sentiments, and perhaps you will not either. I should be very glad to see either of them—better both of them,—or any able Indian in the House of Commons, and would do what little is in my power to help them. But I fear the election of an Indian, if not impossible, will always be a hard matter. There will always be a strong English claimant for an easy, open seat, or for any one where there is a good chance for a Liberal. And I honestly believe that such a man as Knight, Digby, Story, Samuel Smith or Slagg, H. F. Reid or Sir J. Budd Phear, would have more influence, in and out of the House, than a Lal Mohun Ghose or a Dadabhai Naoroji. Dadabhai Naoroji astonished me on the platform, and is always well received. More next week.

Believe me,

Very sincerely yours,

EVANS BELL.

Mr. A. O. Hume, the Father of the Indian Congress, is the correspondent in the ensuing letter. His acumen is shown by the remark that the Doctor was prone to utterances savouring of cynicism. No one gifted with brains and knowledge of mankind can help giving vent to scepticism as regards the real measure of human progress. Mr. Hume has, himself, had abundant reason to question the existence of common gratitude and good faith in men with whom he has been associated in public movements.

From Mr. Allan O. Hume.

Simla, October 5, 1886.

My dear Mr. Mookerjee,—I must indeed have expressed myself badly. *I* think you an "intelligent savage!" I wish we had a few more *such* savages! No, in plain words, judging from *Reis and Rayyet*, what I conceived you to be was a man of high culture, of warm and generous instincts and real patriotism, but at the same time one who, gradually disgusted at the self-seeking, insincerity, and selfishness of the many, had grown sceptical of all real progress in the present generation and had encouraged a cynical spirit. I may very likely be wrong, but this was my reading of your character. It may be that, as we are said all to be prone to do, I judged others by myself, for I feel myself how difficult it is to avoid that scepticism and to bar the way to that cynicism, in face of the boundless professions and infinitesimal performances that I meet with.

Pray don't be unjust or unreasonable. Why on earth should I shrink from you? On the contrary, I would gladly have seen far more of you. Who has got better brains in Calcutta and with whom would I rather consult and discuss matters? I did hope you would come and see me in Calcutta, and I was disappointed that you did not. I should have gone to see you, only I gathered from a note you wrote to Bonnerjee that you were huffed at my writing to you as *Gurujee*, which I only did, not as chaff, but as a pet name, by which Bonnerjee and others often speak of you. Perhaps I had not a right to write thus, but I did it in all friendliness, as I felt towards you.

My dear friend, so far from weighing you in my balance and finding you wanting, I weighed your writings and found they were weighty. Of you personally I know little except that, on two occasions that I met you, you were very pleasant, and fatherly in your manner, though, it seemed to me, full of a half cynical sense of humour, all of which I liked. So far from making enquiries and finding you wanting, I cannot say that I ever heard a single word to your prejudice. I was told and gathered it from your articles, that you had a profound sense of the preponderance of humbug all round us, and though I try hard to drive this feeling out of my own mind, I could not avoid sympathising with you somewhat.

* * *

If you can really think, as you say, that *I* avoided *you* as thinking myself in any way better than yourself, believe me you did me a cruel injustice. With all my sins, my errors of action and omission, all my shortcomings, I have at least this grace that I know what a mass of imperfections I am and do *not* think myself better than my neighbours, and in most cases know myself to be worse. But (I don't know you yet well enough to feel sure what you mean) you may be only chaffing me, and my earnest attempts to clear myself from imaginary charges, imputed by you perhaps merely to take a rise out of me, may only make you laugh. Anyhow, if you are in earnest, I have answered you in earnest. I admire your abilities—to all I have seen and heard of you I am sympathetic. I fear you to be somewhat over cynical, not beyond the deserts of the blatant many, but for the best utilization of your talents in the cause of the country we both love, and if it be so I would fain wean you somewhat from this. But whether I succeed or not, I would gladly know a great deal more of you, and, if you allowed it, number myself amongst your friends.

If you have only been chaffing, then chaff away. I have an unlimited capacity for chaffing and accepting chaff. I am never put out, and, having no dignity to stand on, can always take all good humoured banter in perfect good humour.

Yours very sincerely,

A. O. HUME.

The following letters are nearly all that remain of a voluminous correspondence carried on between the late Mr. Knight, editor of the Calcutta *Statesman*, and my subject. They were, in many respects, kindred spirits, animated both by a profound sense of duty, by a fearlessness of personal consequences and a burning hatred of injustice. The "Rungpur Deer case" is an episode of administration in the interior which it were best to forget.

From Mr. Robert Knight.

The *Statesman*,
3, Chowringhee,
Calcutta, March 17, 1887.

My dear Mookerjee,—You think too much of the simple acknowledgment that I sometimes make of your singular literary powers. In a lawful way I envy you their possession, but I have too deep a contempt for the jealousy which so widely prevails in the Press not to shrink from the feeling itself; and as to permitting it to influence my writings, I have too keen a sense of my accountability to a higher power than man's to dare to give rein to it.

I assure you that it is not I only of the Englishmen you meet, who value *Reis and Rayyet.* I frequently hear the highest testimony to the character of your writings. On Monday night, I sat next to Barnes, the Private Secretary, at the dinner given by the Viceroy to Sir Rivers Thompson, as I was one of the "select party,"—and he expressed his astonishment at your writings. But the fact is becoming generally known, that we have a great writer among us, and I hope the day is not far off when some substantial recognition of the fact will be made. I tell you this because I suspect that you have your moments of depression like myself, and it may be a glass of cold water to refresh you at such time. After all, what is it? We are striving with all our imperfections upon us to do some little good by saying honestly the thought that is in us. It is given to you to say it gracefully and in a winning way. I have ceased to hope that I can even say it in the same happy way, and while I strive to speak the truth from my heart I feel so keenly my shortcomings from my own ideal, that I am very weary of the efforts and would fain never write another line from my sense of the rasping tone in which my nature expresses itself.

Upon the whole, how little effort is there in the Press to speak truthfully! Look at its utterances over the Rungpur Deer case! I do not think I shall say or write much upon it, as all that can be done has been done.

As to the Native Princes, I am strongly

of your mind. They are either denationalized by us, or sent into the Zenana.

Believe me,

Yours very sincerely,

R. KNIGHT.

From Sir Auckland Colvin.

June 13, 1887.

Dear Dr. Mookerjee,—I have to thank you for your two letters of May 10 and 24, and if the heat does not destroy you I hope to have another letter to acknowledge by and bye. Thanks for Mr. Dacosta's pamphlet. I don't think he makes any sufficient allowance for the difficult position of the Government of India which has before it a continual necessity for watchfulness against calamities of seasons on the one hand and, on the other, foreign aggression. It costs money to guard against these dangers. For the last three years, the amount of insurance effected in either direction, and about to be effected, whether by railways or defence works, is immense. This is well, and if it leads to loss of surplus it is a wise use of that surplus.

Nothing has struck me more since I joined this Government than the illiberal tone of the Bengal (including the English or Anglo-Indian) Press.

No credit is given for intelligence, honesty or any other quality. If a council of convicts were driving the coach they could not be more unmannerly spoken of The Bombay Press is reasonable or at least better bred. Cannot the discussion of public affairs be conducted in Calcutta in temperate and courteous terms?

I except your paper. But the * * is ill-bred to a degree which makes its columns as unpleasant as an Allahabad side "gullee" on a June morning. Has Sir Steuart Bayley had a fling of dirt on him yet?

Here we are all quiet. Don't believe any sensational war rumours. They are moonshine, and the frontier difficulty is gradually settling itself. The season so far promises well;

but it is early to cry "safe!" The Silver Commission, I believe, has taken a pronounced bimetallic way. God is great—and we shall see.

I see Sir Henry Harrison is dethroned. How long will Mr. Cotton reign? I was much amused at your description of the so called "Mass Meetings." The imitative genius of the Bengali will bring him into complete discredit if he uses it in this scale and in this direction for long.

Yours truly,

A. COLVIN.

Although his criticisms of men and measures were always incisive, the hurry of journalistic work left Dr. Mookerjee but scanty leisure and sometimes obliged him to trust to general impressions of events. Hence mistakes and misstatements occasionally crept into his paper. But he had none of that pettiness or pride which leads so many journalists to ignore corrections. He accepted them with the best grace and never failed to make an *amende honorable.*

From Mahamahopadhyaya M. C. Nyaratna.

Sanskrit College,
September 13, 1887.

My dear Mookerjee Mahasaya,—I am sorry to see that in the last number of "Reis and Rayyet," the purport of what I said at the Science Association, on Sunday, the 4th instant, when Babu Rabindranath Tagore read a paper on Early Marriage, has been entirely misrepresented. Had the misrepresentation occurred in any of the worthless papers of which we have, perhaps, too many, I would not have cared. But I think I should not let it pass unchallenged when it occurs in a paper like "Reis and Rayyet." You say "Principal Nyaratna, who had been one of the speakers at Sovabazar, avowed himself here a thorough reformer and no respecter of Manu or Yajnyavalka." Now with reference to this statement I have to remark, *first*, that I was not one of the speakers at the Śovabazar meeting. I had only called one of the young speakers, who by the way was a pupil of mine, to order. I did not speak a single word either for or against early marriage. *Secondly,* I did not avow myself at the Science Association meeting "a thorough reformer and no respecter of Manu or Yajnyavalka." I did nothing of the kind. What I said was that the first question to be decided was a question of fact—whether early marriage was not injurious to the community. In the discussion of this question we should confine ourselves to facts as actually observed; and in this observation of facts neither Manu nor Yajnyavalka, neither the Bible nor the Koran could be of much use. I also said that the ascertainment of the question of fact could not be conveniently done at a large public meeting; but should be done at a small committee meeting composed of 14 or 15. If after thorough enquiry by the committee it appeared that early marriage was injurious to the community, then as a Hindu I would propose, if I were one of the committee, to ascertain how far deviation from the custom of early marriage would interfere with the injunction of the shastras. It would similarly be the duty of any Christian or Mahomedan member of such committee to point out how far the matter was consistent with the systems of their respective religions. The first question to decide is a question of fact—whether early marriage is injurious or not. Before that is satisfactorily settled, it is idle to thrust merely religious considerations into the discussion.

That was the drift of what I said. In the columns of the *Sanjibani* you will find a correct version of my speech. The object which I have chiefly in view in addressing this letter to you, is to convince you that you have misunderstood my speech. I shall be amply satisfied if this removed your mistaken impression ;

and it rests entirely with you to decide whether you ought to do anything to remove the wrong impression which you have created in the public mind.

Yours very sincerely,

MAHESH CHANDRA NYARATNA.

Note on the letter by Dr. Mookerjee.—Answered immediately; regret dissatisfaction: but of course a man can only act upon his impressions. Don't see the *Sanjibani.* I shall look into the matter at leisure. One inaccuracy must be corrected as I already see the statement that Nyaratna spoke on the *subject* at Sovabazar. If he has no objection I may print the explanatory part of his present letter with my comments.

From Mr. Robert Knight.

Darjeeling, October 25, 1887.

My dear Sambhu Chunder,—You once said something to me about the "religious" scruples which make Hindu families of distinction so unwilling to have the vaults in which their hoards are secured ever opened. It was my own fault that I did not listen with more attention, but your remark remained in my mind and has so remained ever since. Can you find time to tell me by a note what it exactly was that you said, for I think the point was very interesting as well as important?

I called upon Sir Steuart Bayley a few days ago (the first call I have felt able to make), and we had a long talk about Burdwan, the mass meetings of the rayyets and other subjects. * * *

We spoke of you, and he made a remark that I think you should know. His regret is that you have no "party" behind you. I have felt myself how much influence you could wield as the exponent of a party. Is the formation of such a party impossible? Our conversation confirmed my impression that we have a good man in Sir Steuart Bayley and I should like to support him as far as we can. He introduced the Burdwan adoption question himself, but I shall reserve what he said thereon until we can talk it over together. He seems to think that the matter should go to the High Court, and said (if I understood him rightly) that he sanctioned the adoption, not because he thought it legal but that it would lead to a decision by the High Court which alone could say whether it was so or not.

I hope you are well and that the cold weather will not disagree with you.

Believe me,

Yours very sincerely,

R. KNIGHT.

To Sir Auckland Colvin.

Telegram. November 21, 1887.—After thirty years a Colvin is again on the gubernatorial *guddee.* May God grant him peaceful days and enable him to realize his sire's enlightened programme and advance the wellbeing of the millions of British subjects committed to his charge!

To Sir Auckland Colvin.

December 14, 1887.

My dear Sir Auckland,—I have taken much too long to acknowledge your last and thank you for its offer and its suggestion. The fact is, I have been unwell, suffering from dysentery. Last week it looked rather serious. My physician too, Dr. Sircar, the Sheriff elect of Calcutta, was laid up, and I had to depend on my own resources and on such advice as I could get from one of his assistants. I never had a talk with you on the subject. Probably you think Homœopathy rubbish, but one infinitesimal dose of one medicine and two similar doses of another brought me round, so far at least as to remove the graver symptoms. A radical cure was difficult and could scarcely be expected, depending as it does on many circumstances, on habits of life, &c. For one thing, sedentary pursuits—much thinking without bodily exercise—cannot fail to derange the liver and all the digestive functions. But enough of this unpleasant yarn. I am now thinking of a trip to Madras during the Congress. I am particularly pressed by friends to go, if only for the sake of health. It will depend upon the arrangements for the conduct of the paper. You can understand the difficulty of keeping up a weekly publication of the calibre and reputation of *Reis.* There are so few really good writers among us. Your University graduates are no good. This morning I went to the suburbs to see a friend who used formerly to write in *Reis* and wields a facile and brilliant pen—in prose and in verse—

* * * and he has consented to coach the journal in my absence. A younger gentleman—no youngster though—who has been trained by myself in the art of writing and in the mysteries of journalism has also agreed to do his best.

Sir Steuart Bayley still maintains his place in the heart of his people, and he means to keep it evidently. The Europeans are of course displeased. The Civil Service are furious and the India Government ready to snub him—but of that you know better than I can pretend to do. I am indeed told by one who has access to good sources (his forecast of the Ilbert Bill agitation proved correct), that you supported poor Mr. Beames against the proposition to dismiss or degrade him, your ground being the very intelligible one that Mr. Beames brought on him the enmity of the natives by his outspoken evidence before the Public Service Commission. I do not know how you will like this news, but I thought it my duty to tell it. I dare say you expect me to keep you informed of anything I hear about you. * * It is not cold here yet—that is, December weather. In your *Raj* it must be delightful now, possibly uncomfortable.

Yours very sincerely,

SAMBHU C. MOOKERJEE.

To Sir Auckland Colvin.

1, Uckoor Dutt's Lane,
Calcutta, December 28, 1887.

Dear Sir Auckland,— * *

I am sure you are making a happy X'mas of it at your capital in the plains: a merry one might be too much of a good thing at this time of life. I wish you a pleasant and prosperous coming year and may your days be long and blessed with a continuance of health and enjoyment! The English Christmas is a poor thing in Lower Bengal. Is it any better in Upper India, I wonder? Although there is no snow in the plains, the weather is cold enough to make a fire pleasant. In the olden days when the E. I. Railway itself burned wood, I suppose the British exiles were reminded of their Christmas Log at Home.

I am delighted to hear from the N.-W. P. of the fine impression you have made on the people. You are already on the high road to popularity. With your great abilities, your knowledge of the country, and your tact, I never doubted of your success, if you allowed them play and relied upon yourself. But it is satisfactory to know of the beginning of the consummation. Think not that I value the vulgar applause that is earned at the sacrifice of one's sense of duty and the right. My whole career (such as it has been) is proof enough that I do not. If popularity comes in due course from the performance of honest work, it is pedantry and the vanity of a foolish squeamishness to spurn it. I confess I had some little misgivings on the point. But enough of this strain which might lead to the miserable *rôle* of the "candid friend."

I am meditating a visit to the Upper Provinces in search of health. I may surprise you in the course of your tour. * *

Yours sincerely,

SAMBHU C. MOOKERJEE.

To Sir Auckland Colvin.

January 19, 1888.

My dear Sir Auckland,—If I did not know how engrossed you were at the outset of your heavy charge, I should be tempted to enquire what was the matter with you, not having heard from you for a long time. Although your movements are now among the more urgent topics of journalism, and although you have been pretty much before the public, it is just possible that you are not in the best health and spirits. At all events, my own condition of feebleness leads me to this train of thought. It would be a relief to be assured that you are the victim of nothing more formidable than the overloyal attentions of my old friend Moonshee Newul Kishore and the Reises of Lucknow and of the Urdu eloquence of the *Fesana Ajáeb* type.

As I have hinted, I have not been well myself. Indeed, I had an attack of cholerine, as I must now call it, God having permitted me to write of it. My health had been bad for a considerable time and I was contemplating a change—a hint of which I believe I gave in one of my letters—when this attack intervened. At one time I thought of going to Madras to the Congress, to see how they ordered the matter down South and keep our Boys of Bengal in check, particularly in matters of social discipline. But it was not to be. I could not get a P. O. or other presumably safe steamer, and I would not form part of the cargo of Babudom of all castes in charge of Thomas Cook and Son. But enough of all this.

I see that the *Hindoo Patriot* has tackled you in your manifesto. The writer is, I am glad to observe, respectful in tone, though he does not spare the weak point in the address. The *Dnyan Prakash* of Poona does not take up anything like a hypercritical attitude but welcomes the speech as a frank and manly utterance of good intentions and good advice from a liberal ruler.

Yours sincerely,

SAMBHU C. MOOKERJEE.

From the Earl of Rosebery.

Dalmney Park,

Edinburgh, January 26, 1888.

Sir,—I remember our conversation at Calcutta very well, and am gratified that you have not forgotten me. I am grateful to you for the book of travels which I have had not time to read since it arrived two days ago, but which I have put on my table for perusal. If it is written with the same general pleasantry as your letter to me, I shall have reason to thank you still more.

Let me also acknowledge *Reis and Rayyet* which reaches me from time to time, and which I often look at.

I am sorry that your caste does not allow of your crossing the sea, but I shall hope to set eyes on you again in India, a country

I should only be too happy to revisit.

With all good wishes, believe me,

Yours, &c.,

ROSEBERY.

From Colonel R. D. Osborn.

20, Winchester Road,
South Hampstead,
February 16, 1888.

My dear Sir,—I have to acknowledge with many thanks your present of your "Travels in Bengal." I have read the little book with a great deal of pleasure. It is charmingly written, and my only regret is that you have not entered into more copious details. There is no part of India more interesting historically and also in its present condition than Eastern Bengal, and I should have been glad had you told us a great deal more about the Mahomedan population of that part of the world. I have, of course, been long familiar with your name and with much of your writing, and I have an impression—confirmed by the reading of these "Travels"—that you could, if you tried, write a good novel of Native Life—such a story, for example, as that delightful "Poison Tree." What we stand so sorely in need of from men possessing so complete a command of English as yourself, are pictures of those more intimate aspects of Native Life which, so long as Hindus are Hindus, must remain unknown to Englishmen. I wish, if you do not feel that a novel is in your way, that you would give us a series of pictures of Native Interiors drawn from the life in Bengal somewhat after the manner of Mr. Malabari's "Gujrat and the Gujratis." It would be the doing of a real service to both countries. I, as you know, have spent many years in India, and yet, as regards Indian domesticities, I feel I know about as much of what exists on the other side of the world, and I am convinced that it is this ignorance which is largely responsible for the gulf which divides the Englishman from the Indian.

I was amused by your remarks in the preface on the translation of the ode from Hafez, because, years ago when I was studying Persian, I tried my hand at translating that very ode and, like my predecessors, had to give up "the mole on the cheek" as unmanageable. I take it that Hafez meant to glorify the loveliness of the person he was celebrating (who, I fear, was of the male sex) by stating that even for a defect he would not give &c., &c.; but "black mole on his cheek" is too long a phrase to be rendered within the compass of a verse. However my version—though I say it that should not—is better, because more terse than all preceding attempts that I know of. I transcribe two verses of it, as they may amuse you—

O! if that sweet Shirazee girl
Would take my heart in hand,

I'd give Bokhara for a *kiss*
 And the wealth of Samarkand.

O! Sakee fill the cup for me—
See Heav'n, alas! 'tis sad—
Musella's walks we shall not see,
Nor the streams of Roknabad.

That second stanza is a most characteristic one, instinct with that gay profanity which gives so much charm and sprightliness to the poetry of the great Persian. Here is another verse from another ode which has much the same flavour—

The joys of the eight heavens meet
"About the beggar in your street,
The prisoner of your charms is free
Of this world and the world to be."

However I am not writing about Hafez, but your book. So I will stop before I am fairly involved in a dissertation.

Repeating my thanks for the pleasure you have given me, I remain,

Yours very truly,

ROBERT D. OSBORN.

To His Excellency the Earl of Dufferin.

March 13, 1888.

My Lord,—At our conversation of the other day, you were pleased to offer to present to me your celebrated book on your Arctic Voyage of youthful days. In expressing my thanks for the honour, I took the opportunity of mentioning a little book of Travels and Voyages (such as they were) of my own just out, and expressed the gratification I would feel if your Lordship should accept my humble present of a copy. Your Lordship not only signified your willingness, but was so good as to compliment me by treating the matter as one of exchange between authors.

Here, then, is my *nuzzur.* It is worth no more, if so much ; but then almost any *bagatelle* is allowable for a *nuzzer*, specially from Brahmans who are notoriously deficient in the world's goods. That deficiency is, of course, due to the shabby treatment they receive, empty respect only being usually their portion. According to a proverb, the blind cow is disposed of by present to a Brahman. What wonder that etiquette should rule it sufficient, and even proper, for a Brahman to approach Power, or the Presence itself, with an offering of a green *bael* or a sour mango!

I have need to make some apology for taking your Lordship at your word. There is an obvious presumption in a native of India who has not been educated in England nor has resided there, who has not had the advantage of mixing in such European society as exists in this country, attempting a book of any pretensions in so difficult and rich and growing a language as the English. And then for such a man to appear as an author before an accomplished master of the language whose felicity of style is so marvellous! Above all, how absurd for me who has never crossed salt water, to try to interest, with the story of my amazement at the broad reaches of the river Megna and my bewilderment in the marshes of Tippera, the knight of the sea who, early in the century, planted his flag in the adamantine ice in the neighbourhood of the Pole! In fine, both in subject and treatment, there is a striking sense of descent from the sublime to the ridiculous, from the "Letters from High Latitudes" to the Diary of business tours between Calcutta and Independent Tippera.

I can think of no other claim of my book on your Lordship's attention than as describing a part of the dominions under your rule which has been wholly neglected by travellers and authors. It has, however, one general claim on all classes of readers on which even the writer himself may insist without reproach. It is short. A great book must have been a great evil even in the days of the Patriarchs. How much more so in these overburdened times! Brevity is a quality which must specially recommend itself to men in your Lordship's position. If my *Travels* should ever tempt your Lordship on that ground, may I hope to be favoured with your opinion and suggestions for improvement?

I see that I have made up the shortness of my book by the length of this introductory letter. I beg your Lordship's pardon for presuming to occupy so much of your valuable time.

I have the honour to subscribe myself,

My Lord,

Your most humble and faithful servant,

SAMBHU C. MOOKERJEE.

To His Excellency the Earl of Dufferin.

March 26, 1888.

My Lord,—The next afternoon after receipt of your kind note, I had, at Lady Dufferin's Garden Party, an opportunity of which I availed myself of thanking you in person for it and for the interesting present which enhanced the value, great as it was by itself, of the gracious acknowledgment of my booklet rather than book of Travels in Bengal. Still a record of my sense of the favour was, I thought, due, and I was only waiting for my photographic likeness for submission for your Lordship's acceptance. But I have for this waited in vain. There are European establishments in plenty, some between Government House and this, but I was looking out for a competent native photographer, as from the conversation I had with your Lordship I knew you would prefer a specimen of genuine Indian Art. For myself, the art might make the object more acceptable and worthy of your Lordship's collections. I do not know whether they would care to take me at the Art School—I do not know the Principal. I shall no doubt be able to send a photograph to your Lordship at Simla. Old Gangadhar Dey, who has painted me in oil, is not a bad photographer, but he has no proper studio. Meanwhile, time presses and I cannot let your

Lordship leave Calcutta without expressing my sense of the high honour you have done me by your letter and the present of your famous book inscribed with your autograph, and of your noble likeness so well taken by the Italian establishment in Bombay. If it were possible for me to forget the great kindness you have ever shown me, since the moment that, by your own condescension, I became known to your Lordship, these will always bring your Lordship to mind and keep me to my duty. But I must not weary you any further, and so, with sentiments of great respect and thankfulness,

I beg to subscribe myself,

My Lord,

Your Lordship's obedient humble servant,

SAMBHU C. MOOKERJEE.

To His Excellency the Earl of Dufferin.

May 1, 1888.

My Lord,—I take much blame upon myself for not having, since your Lordship's departure from Calcutta, availed myself of the honour of your very kind permission to write to you. For one reason, I had some hope of meeting your Lordship again in the North. My health has long needed a change, and I have longed to see the famed vale of Cashmere. A run to Cashmere during the viceregal visit was recommended to me as an opportunity of killing two birds with one stone. There would be grand doings to report for the paper, thought I, and a little book on Cashmere—described for the first time from the point of view of a native of India—might eventually be the result. If Cashmere did not supply sufficient matter for a volume, my travels in the Punjab and the N.-W. Provinces, which I meant to take in on my way back, would meet the deficiency. Thus I made arrangements and asked a friend—the same accomplished gentleman who acted for me during my last trip to Tippera in 1884—to take charge of the paper. But my hopes were dashed to the ground when, in consequence of sickness in the country, your Lordship abandoned your trip. They are now reviving under the news that your Lordship meditates a tour in autumn—"the fall," as you would probably have said in Canada. In that case, I shall try again, with your Lordship's permission.

We were cut up by the Simla telegram in the *Indian Daily News* announcing your departure in August, if not earlier. It seemed improbable. In the event of any unforeseen turn of affairs, I was in some hopes that your Lordship would be so good as to tell Sir D. Mackenzie Wallace to wire me a line. I, therefore, fully expected the other morning papers next day to contradict the news. None did so, and I saw that the statement in the *Indian Daily News* was having an undesirable effect on the community. In order to be able to contradict it and learn the true facts, I telegraphed to Sir Donald and got his answer on Saturday evening in time for my paper. On Monday, the contradiction appeared in the *Englishman* and the *Indian Daily News.* I believe the Private Secretary wired to them at the same time that he telegraphed to me.

The events of the day are the falls of Luchman Das in Cashmere and Abdool Huq in Hyderabad. The former is comparatively a local sensation. The latter is not only the talk of the whole British world but affects the interests—in purse and in character—of many well-known and some eminent men in both countries—I mean India and Great Britain. I am glad that the action of the Government has been such as to commend itself to the approbation of all disinterested men. Without the consent of that Government, the Nizam would not have ventured on the decisive course he has taken. It was a bold thing, (your Lordship will, I trust, pardon my presumptuous utterance) in the Government to sanction such a proceeding. But it was a righteous thing. And that is consolation enough. There is unhappily no other. It was still more bold to support the demand in the House of Commons for a Parliamentary Committee of Inquiry. As a line of action foreign to the disposition and traditions of the Indian Government and the India Office, it must have startled the whole official class. It will, I am afraid, create many influential enemies who, not content with the savings of their splendid Indian salaries, try in their retirement or partial retirement in England to make as much as they can out of the helplessness of Native States. I rejoice that the Government has acted with spirit and perfect frankness. It has vindicated its purity and raised immensely the moral prestige of England in the East.

From a Parliamentary point of view I think this departure has been proper. It shows a just appreciation of the times. It is forty years since Louis Kossuth thundered against Secret Diplomacy as the curse of Europe. He was then carried away by his sense of wrong to himself and his country from the facility with which, unknown to their peoples, the Hapsburgs and Romanoffs and the other sovereign tribes carried on their intrigues against the nationalities. Since then he has learnt better, his own memoirs showing how he adopted the same methods of his old enemies and even stooped to be the agent of crowned heads in secret negociations. But democracy is unfavourable to secrecy. It is enough that its leaders still admit the necessity of secrecy, at least in the earlier stages of negociation. But they might find it difficult to control the forces under them if statesmen continued to put forward imaginary state reasons in order to evade legitimate enquiry at every turn. There is wisdom as well as honesty in the attitude of your Lordship's

Government. * * *

I am afraid I have taken too much advantage of your Lordship's kindness in inflicting such a long rigmarole. I rely on your goodness for pardon.

I remain,

With the greatest respect,

My Lord,

Your Lordship's most obedient humble servant,

SAMBHU C. MOOKERJEE.

From Sir Lepel Griffin.

The Residency,

Indore, February 3, 1888.

Dear Sir,—I am much obliged to you for your polite and friendly letter, and I need not tell you that your estimate of the attacks made upon me by the (Anglo-) Bengalee Press is a just one, as is your statement of the source from which they proceed. The * * * is directly subsidized by the ex-Nawab * * , who supplies it with papers and information from the

Durbar Office. These are twisted to suit the tastes of the person who pays for them. I have been disinclined to take any action personally in the matter, as there is no single charge which has been made against me which is not false and malicious. Whether the Government, who are fully cognisant of all my actions and who have as fully approved of them, will take any action against these paid libellers I know not. There has been scarcely an issue of the * * * published for months on which a criminal prosecution for libel might not be successfully instituted. I have, however, no doubt that the Government will take proper measures to vindicate my character and their own.

The *Asiatic Quarterly* does not profess to have any politics and is quite open to well-written articles on any subject if they be of general public interest, and if you send me the article in question, I will tell you at an early date whether it is suited to the Review.

Yours truly,

LEPEL GRIFFIN.

To Sir Donald Mackenzie Wallace.

March 24, 1888.

My dear Sir Donald,—Sir Lepel Griffin is a naughty old boy to put the whole Press on the wrong scent by his announcement that he was about to depose another ruling prince in Central India. After the attacks the *Pioneer* had of late been levelling against Holkar, people naturally jumped to the conclusion that Indore's turn had come. That shows the state of feeling of the country in these matters, and Government would be wise in treating with due respect the anxiety of the people with regard to the remaining vestiges of autonomous rule in India and their readiness to take instant alarm at the slightest appearance of danger.

But I am again being led into my unhappy

discursive vein. My object in writing is to make sure before I bring out my paper as to which prince was doomed. Sir Auckland Colvin told me it was a petty chief whose name he could not remember. Afterwards I heard from another source that it was Dewas. And that is the truth, I take it. But then, which Dewas? There are, I believe, two branches of the family, the senior and the junior. And for what offence? And what are the coming arrangements?

I would not have ventured to put these questions without encouragement from above. You will rememember how, whenever I went to pay my respects as a representative of the subject race to the grand depository of State Secrets, I was content to discuss the weather and other equally momentous topics, finding no disposition in you to allude to the subjects of policy or administration which might be occupying our minds most at the moment. Of course, you could not be communicative without orders and there might be danger in mere listening, not to say discussing. I am bound to acknowledge His Excellency's frank courtesy in himself encouraging me to talk and even ask questions. He has offered to give any information or explanation of what might be obscure. And he has referred me to your good self as accessible at all hours.

I write all this in order to expedite your reply if possible. I know how difficult it is to get anything out of officials in your position. It was not without a hard struggle and a long, long delay that I could get last night a copy of the Viceroy's reply from Mr. Panioty, to whom you referred me. And as you must be starting soon for Uttarpara, if you waited for His Excellency's express permission before writing to me, I could not possibly make use of the information this week.

I remain, my dear Sir Donald,

Yours sincerely,

SAMBHU C. MOOKERJEE.

To Sir Auckland Colvin.

May 24, 1888.

My dear Sir Auckland,—It is so long since I dropped correspondence that I am ashamed and at a loss how to begin again. On your part the duties of a supreme office left you little inclination to think of, and less leisure to write to poor Mookerjee, unless Etiquette —that minor tyrant of civilized life—had some little share in preventing you from calling me to account for my lâches yourself. How I came not to write ever since our cordial parting at Government House in this city, is a wonder and not quite easy to explain at this distance. Shall I plead the weather? You had a taste of the purgatory too, I believe, before you made for the Kumaon hills. Health would be a better excuse, but I was never so ill as to be disabled from correspondence. As far as I recollect at this moment I meditated a surprise, coming suddenly *in propia persona* upon you, on a tour for health, having had no change for years. For a single-handed editor, it is easier to indulge visions of a Long Vacation than to realize them. I was delayed in making arrangements for the office. Meanwhile, the dream developed into a vision of the Vale of Cashmere. I would kill more than two birds with one stone. By one expenditure I would do Cashmere, improve my health, enjoy grand *tamashas*, report for my paper, and obtain the *nucleus* of a book, provided I was in the Valley during the Viceroy's visit. All these fond reflections were dashed to the ground by the cholera which scared Lord Dufferin away from his intended tour. Then, as a last resource, I thought there might be inspiring scenes and picturesque ceremonials at the Rampore Investiture, but still thought it prudent to enquire before undertaking a long journey in fearful weather. Your telegram from Lucknow gave the quietus to my roving fancy. But at this rate my preface will leave no room for my book. So I must plunge *in medias res.*

What you predicted respecting the attitude of the native press towards Sir Steuart Bayley is about coming to pass. The * *, the true representative of the loud unthinking mass of native politicians, has already hinted that Sir Steuart is worse than Sir Rivers Thompson, and the latter is a sort of Mephistopheles in the native mind—a miserable psalm-singing political sinner. This revulsion of feeling is due to the Tangail Resolution, but chiefly to the Calcutta Municipality Bill.

But how comes the prophet to fail in wisdom in his own case? The sagacity to make a correct forecast of a brother ruler ought to be a preservative against one's own liabilities. I deeply lament the estrangement between yourself and the Nationalist party. I am sure you have *done* nothing to cause it; but couldn't you, veteran as you are in governing, in diplomacy as in administration, prevent it, if you cared enough? Our people—the Boys of the Period, in the Press and on the platform—are rather difficult to please. I myself don't. But I don't care. My first duty is to my country and to truth. Though a Liberal by education, I am a thorough Oriental for a' that. Representative of the old Rishis, I am by instinct Conservative. I am deliberately of opinion that the safety of our country lies, and will lie for many many years to come, in subjection and cordial loyalty to Britain. I do not believe in a French Revolution for India. Your business is to rule, to keep all parties straight, and to satisfy all, if possible. It is not so impossible for you. More anon.

Yours sincerely,

SAMBHU C. MOOKERJEE.

From Sir Auckland Colvin.

Government House,
Naini-Tal, June 22, 1888.

Dear Dr. Mookerjee,—Your letter of 24th May

is unanswered, and as I see in the papers that the Calcutta sun is slowly consuming the Calcutta city, I propose to temper your last hours by a few words from these cooler regions. Not but that what we too are in a dust haze, slowly drifting through breathless hour into the rainy months ahead of us.

We are very quiet at present. * *

Have you seen a very good article by George Curzon in the *Nineteenth Century* on the Scientific Frontier? It is excellent and gives one very precise and accurate information as to the measures which have been taken in the last three years to strengthen the frontier. It is well worth re-publishing in your paper.

So Sir Steuart Bayley is losing popularity! Popularity is an accident. I would not do anything deliberately to throw it away; but I would not go out of my way to secure it, if the price of securing it was going out of the way I believed the necessary one.

I hope you are keeping well in spite

of the heat. What is the last Calcutta sensation?

Yours very truly,

A. COLVIN.

To His Excellency the Earl of Dufferin.

Calcutta, June 20, 1888.

My Lord,—I would have liked to write sooner, the more so as some points in your Lordship's most kind and interesting letter of the 17th May seemed to require an answer, but that I was anxious to avoid all appearance of taking undue advantage. In India we have to be very careful, we of the subject race in particular. The immediate impulse to break silence today is supplied by the news abroad that your Lordship is going to Cashmere after all in October, and to ascertain if that is true.

The evidence before the Parliamentary Committee must cause your Lordship no little surprise. It not only shows the perfunctory, easy-going fashion in which high officials perform their duties, but also the greed which characterizes so many who have made their fortunes and virtually retired from active life. I hope some good will come out of the unpleasant revelations. It ought at any rate to open the eyes of Parliament and the public to the corruption that taints the administration at every stage. That corruption is universal, though certainly not so barefaced as before the Government of Lord W. Bentinck—who suppressed what was called the *Dalee* system—to say nothing of the days of Clive and Hastings and the "Nabobs." The root of the evil lies in the tribal *personnel* of the Indian services. The destruction of Haileybury and Addiscombe and throwing open of the services to public competition would, it was hoped, improve their *morale*. But under the new system, the old Indian families still maintain their preponderance, while the fresh admissions soon imbibe the *esprit de corps* of the existing body. "Society" winks at its members profiting at the expense of Government, and even enjoys their fleecing Natives. It is a pity that Europeans do not associate with native gentlemen of education and character, or they might at one time or another hear the names of the black sheep in the services and the contempt in which they are held. In the absence of any healthy intercourse between the two races, the native press, whatever its failings, undoubtedly performs a particularly important function. That press has been a more effectual check than almost any other agency. Of course, the distance at which its conductors are kept from all sources of authentic information and, above all, from the better intellectual and moral influences of European society, cripples its capacity for usefulness. Still, when Europeans are irritated, and justly irritated, by the sins of the Native Press, and denounce it for its manifold imperfections and faults, it is but just to remember the important function it fulfils or essays to fulfil, in a country without recognized representative institutions—a dependency of a distant Power. Innumerable instances might be adduced, over and above *a priori* arguments, to prove the actual benefit of our imperfect Press. * * *

The terror naturally inspired by it in those whose practices will not bear scrutiny is the chief cause of the passionate animosity towards the Press of many Anglo-Indians. If, instead, they took more kindly to it, they would do better, to themselves as to those within their influence. The pity is that they do not care to study the press. Without taking the trouble to know, they take a violent prejudice against it. All native papers are equally and infinitely bad in the opinion of those who never look at any. There are papers and papers, however, and if officials made their choice and habitually consulted the more reputable organs of native thought, they would be saved a good deal of indiscretion and save themselves and Government trouble. It is in the complete absence of touch with the native population that the generality of officers in the civil and political administration so lamentably fail. The Governments themselves are in these days advanced enough to recognize the power and usefulness of native opinion, but the rank and file of officialdom still persist in ignorance and disregard of it. * * * Our paper is the only one that has had the courage and honesty to notice the charge of bribery and corruption against the Collector of Calcutta, now under investigation. * * * A native Indian journal may be regarded by journalists and politicians in England and even quoted in Parliament, yet Indian officers may be unfamiliar with its very name. It is the natives that entirely support the native press. That is natural and proper, but it ought not to be wholly so. This limitation of constituency has the effect of intensifying the partizanship of the press and gradually estranging both press and people from Government and the Europeans. A great deal of unnecessary friction of late years is due to this cause. I think heads of Government might, in a quiet way, specially in their tours, enquire into the sources of information of officials, what native gentlemen of light and leading they see, which papers they consult, &c. The subject is a delicate one, and being myself interested I am not so sure whether my own judgment is so unclouded that I could suggest any regular official step. Your Lordship might know better. But the political Agencies are so ill-manned and are situated so far from all sources of healthy influence and from all knowledge of general Indian opinion, that a return may be called for of the publications received at every such office of whatever dignity or insignificance.

* * *

The heat is unprecedented, and simply intolerable—even for us of the soil. Verily, the agitation against the "Exodus" has been avenged!

I remain, with great esteem, my dear Lord,

Yours sincerely,

SAMBHU C. MOOKERJEE.

To His Excellency the Earl of Dufferin.

1, Uckoor Dutt's Lane,
Calcutta, October 2, 1888.

My Lord,—Months have elapsed since I last had had the pleasure and privilege of addressing your Lordship. My health has not been good. I have been much too long confined at a stretch to this Calcutta atmosphere. Still, as I found time for less important things, I could certainly make time for a correspondence which, besides the honour of it, gave me the inestimable advantage of bringing me, an unofficial politician at best, to the foot of the fountain of British Policy and political action in the East. But I was afraid of overdoing it. It were a shame to have taken advantage of such a kindness. So much by way of explanation—which is always embarrassing to the giver and tedious to the receiver.

After this length of time, I may be excused for desire for knowing the true state of your Lordship's health. At one time the rumours in Calcutta European society caused considerable anxiety. Whatever foundation there may have been for it, I trust all is now right. It is a pity your Lordship has given up the idea of going to Cashmere. I need scarcely say with what pleasure I look forward to your coming again to Calcutta.

* * *

There is great anxiety in Gwalior about the Presidency, specially since Mr. Henvey's departure from Simla. It was expected that the minor Prince's grandfather would be confirmed in the office, but no orders having followed, the rumour of a British Superintendence has revived. I hope no such move is in contemplation. The public are already prone enough to believe that Government are intent on a policy of anglicisation. That may be considered a little matter, but it is not expedient to alienate the feelings of the great Mahratta State. Nor would the forcing on it of an English Vizier be consistent with the wise policy of restoring the fort of Gwalior.

*　　　*　　　*

I have the honour to remain, my Lord,
With sincere esteem and humble attachment,
Yours sincerely,
SAMBHU C. MOOKERJEE.

To Sir Donald Mackenzie Wallace.

July 3, 1888.

My dear Wallace,—I hear the temperature of Simla this season is much too high for comfort. On the 22nd June, Sir Auckland Colvin wrote from Naini-Tal to say that they too were in a dust haze. Down here the heat was frightful, and all the more intolerable for being long continued. But God is gracious and forsakes not his own. The most tedious night is exhausted after all, and at last morrow comes. And so the monsoon has finally burst in right earnest. It is raining delightfully. All nature is dancing again with life. By the bye, have you ever seen the rains in the Tropics? Few things to my mind are so charming as a copious persistent downpour, though of course continual repetition makes a nuisance of it, as of every other thing.

Now I have submitted to the inexorable law of your society by descanting on the weather, I may turn to business.

And first of the subject nearest to us Ditchers—the Municipality Bill which awaits viceregal sanction. I do not see how, without insulting the Chairman of the Corporation, and the Legislature, and the Bengal Government, the oppositionists can be gratified. I hear the plea of absence of jurisdiction in the Council to alter the boundaries has been referred to the Advocate General. The opposition to the measure in native society is universal. There is a feeling of consternation at the prospect of its becoming law. And there is justification enough for it. The Bill passed is revolutionary as I plainly said in *Reis*, notwithstanding my personal kindness for Sir Henry Harrison and Dr. Simpson, and though personally I rather like the sanitary provisions, feeling that some stiff dose is required to modify the arrangements of Indian homes and domestic organization. The idea of inquisition into the family sanctum by outsiders is horrible to the Oriental mind I confess I am no exception. A few years back, my servants at my family house at Baranagore, in the north suburban town, thrashed some surveyor who, armed with an order of Government, had trespassed into the "Gardens of the Seraglio" of the poor Brahman, and I supported them. The Survey Department complained to the head of the District and the Police were set upon me. The District Superintendent himself came, but instead of coming to me he sent for me in the Police way and I did not go. Probably his instructions were to come to me, so after long waiting in the road under the sun he at last came to my house. Instead, however, of coming to my room, as I had asked him to do through his Inspector, he remained downstairs in the courtyard which he filled with his rabble and the rabble of the street in a sort of enquiry that he pretended to hold, thinking perhaps he had done me as much honour as he could by invading my house and the peace of my family with his myrmidons, and that my turn was then to go down on all fours before the Majesty of the Police. I had a great mind to drive out the impudent beggar for his noisy demonstration, but I was not strong enough and thought one criminal case was enough at a time. The D. S. of course vowed vengeance and soon proceedings were instituted in the name of the Queen against the rebel, and my valet was fined, after no little anxiety and expense to me. There was not the slightest possibility of implicating me personally in the business. I was not on the scene, and my face is not familiar to the Police of Baranagore where I rarely go, or they would have named me a defendant in view of annoying me. If, instead of wasting several hours in the court of my house, the officer had come and asked me, he would have got all the facts that had come to my notice and my servants would have been open to prosecution all the same. I have gone into all this detail to give you and His Excellency an idea of how matters are ordered in this blessed country. Only the other day, in my house at Calcutta, a surveyor and his men came and tried to break into it in the discharge of their duty by order of Government. They were naturally repulsed by my servant—the same who had guarded his master's honour at Baranagore and had suffered for it (for though his fine was paid by me as well as his counsel found, he suffered enough anxiety and trouble.) The strangers were impertinent, saying they had the *Sircar's hookum* and were entering all zenanas, but my man was firm and said that the *dustoor* in that family was different from those they had hitherto visited. They retired that day, but came again and again with the same object, their insolence rather increasing at every visit. On two occasions I overheard from my office what was going on. And again there seemed a prospect of my servant getting into trouble. But those who have a nice sense of honour cannot restrain themselves. Notwithstanding the credentials of the surveying party, the pretension to enter my zenana seemed such an insult that when the matter was reported to me I told them to call again, after they had been several times before, and when they came again their bearing so vexed me that I was near committing myself as a "mild Hindu" Wat Tyler. And in point of fact I am naturally a very mild man, as I believe most brave men are. That will give you the feeling in such matters. It is different with the natives who have returned from England, but they do not represent the people, in these matters at any rate. I shall not be surprised if this measure brought Government into trouble.

There is only one way in which the conflicting interests might be in some measure harmonised, but it will easily suggest itself to His Excellency and, as I have already taken up too much space in this matter, I pass on to others.

What are the reports about the new Dewan of Indore? * * *

Have you noticed the allegation that the Resident took the Maharaja of Mysore to task for taking an interest in the National Congress and paying a thousand rupees towards the expenses of that held at Madras ? Is it possible ?

You have doubtless seen the younger ——'s letter on his and his father's connection with the Residency of Hyderabad. What an ass !

Is it true that the Government of India are agreed and have recommended the reconstitution of the Legislative Councils on a representative basis ?

This letter was commenced late last night. I read in the papers today that there is to be an operation on the Viceroy's hand. What is the matter ? Nothing serious, I hope.

Yours very sincerely,

SAMBHU C. MOOKERJEE.

P.S.—Is the Hyderabad Committee considered to have worked satisfactorily ? They seem to be jubilitating in the Deccan as if a great victory has been won or a gold mine discovered. * *

S. C. M.

From Sir Donald Mackenzie Wallace.

Private Secretary's Office,
Viceregal Lodge,
Simla, July 6, 1888.

Dear Mr. Mookerjee,—I am directed by the Viceroy to acknowledge with thanks the receipt of your letter of the 20th June. His Excellency has read it with much interest and intended to reply to it at some length, but his time is at present so fully occupied that I think there is very little chance of his being able to carry out his intention. You can readily understand that a Viceroy's official duties leave him very little time for the friendly discussion of big questions in private letters.

* * *

As for the native press, if I began to discuss that subject I should be in danger of writing a volume. Suffice it to say that *here* it is not by any means so neglected and ignored as you seem to suppose and that whilst its follies and sins are deplored, its merits and services are duly recognized. As yet it is still in its infancy, and we may hope that its wisdom and public usefulness will increase with its years.

Yours sincerely,

DONALD MACKENZIE WALLACE.

P. S.—I have just noticed with regret in the *Reis and Rayyet* an attack on my worthy and esteemed assistant, Mr. Panioty. I cannot suppose that it is from your pen, because it displays a personal animosity to which your pen, so far as I know it, is a stranger. Perhaps some day when we get down to Calcutta you will honour the premises with a visit and judge for yourself. For the lease of the premises it is I who am responsible and I flatter myself I made a very good bargain. I was careful however whilst securing the benefits for my successor not to bind him in the matter. He cannot be ejected or have the rent raised on him, but he may give up the premises, if he likes, on reasonable notice being given to the proprietor. If he can find at the same price anything half as suitable as regards locality and other conveniences he will be more fortunate than I have been, and I trust for his own sake and for the sake of the public interests that he may be able to retain Mr. Panioty's services.

In a paragraph in the same number I notice it is said: "We mean to return to the subject." If it is intended to make an onslaught on the leasing of present premises, it is at me and not at Mr. Panioty that the shafts should be directed.

D. M. W.

To Sir Auckland Colvin.

Calcutta, December 18, 1888.

My dear Sir Auckland,—Pray excuse me this delay in entering epistolary appearance. It were foolish in one in my situation to plead to you want of leisure, seeing how much you have always to do and how you manage to do it all, but it has been a very busy time with me, so much so that I have not been able to give the necessary amount of attention to my paper. Last week, I was glad enough to ask at the last moment another to do the welcome "leader" and had not time to give it the finishing strokes to rescue it from the commonplace, being engaged on the other articles, one written to help the poor tenantry of the Midnapore estate of the Burdwan Raj and the other at the particular request of friends. A part of the delay was caused by the mysterious disappearance—to use the dialect of the Agony column of British newspapers—of my bunch of keys of my correspondence boxes (I never leave your letters and such like papers on the table but always keep them under lock and key) for more than a week. Thank God the Prodigal has returned home safe and sound, though after infinite trouble taken in vain. Office and sleeping apartments and sitting room and library and zenana were all ransacked—all my books and papers and things overhauled for the missing keys in vain. They turned up accidentally on Monday. You have no idea of the crowded state of my place and cannot sympathise with me for the disturbance caused by the search. I may here mention that Mr. William Digby, the Congress agent in England, came to see me by appointment on Monday. The first remark he made, "after compliments," was that he found me in just the kind of apartment he had pictured me occupying in his mind,—surrounded by books and papers and prints—books on the table, books, &c. on the side-table and shelves, books in heaps lying on the floor, pictures on the wall, unframed paintings laid against the wall from the floor. I wonder what he thought of the smoking apparatuses of sorts which were lying about, all different from the snake-piped Jeypore *hookah* from which I was drawing the odoriferous fumes of tobacco doctored with all the spices of Araby the Blest and the Farther East.

Your letter to Mr. Hume is brilliant and incisive. Its main drift is sound and its force irresistible. In despair the Congressists gave out that the Viceroy had disowned you, but at last it transpired at the St. Andrew's Dinner that Lord Dufferin had taken your cue. He paid you an unusual compliment, very honourable to him, by quoting you in his historic oration. His peroration is enriched by one of your best passages. I was talking on the subject in private with him and said that you might have made your case stronger and he seemed to agree, but in what view I could not ascertain. You had no assistance, evidently. * * *

Now that the session is at hand, I feel that I ought to go and see the Congress, the more so as after the event I could not rely on anybody's report. The difficulty is to find accommodation. I cannot stop at Lowther Castle, and would not live there, huddled together with so many, even if I went as a delegate. All my friends are mad about the Congress and Congressists, besides all have been long since engaged. If I asked, perhaps I could get a separate tent away from the bustle of our Indian Runnymede, but I would not ask Hume or Bonnerjee. I am making some negociations. Should they succeed, I expect to pass some days with you, if you are in an accessible country.

Yours sincerely,

SAMBHU C. MOOKERJEE.

Whenever Dr. Mookerjee noticed a piece of superior writing in any of the papers, he tried to unearth the author. He often said that we had so few writers amongst us that any one who discovered power above the average should be sought out and encouraged. In this way he made the acquaintance of many novices and exhorted them to persevere. His advice to such was to endeavour to express themselves neatly, without using sesquipedalian words; and above all to avoid quotations from the British poets. The excision of superfluous words in a sentence was the foremost characteristic of a good style. He was equally averse to the use of phrases from the Greek and Latin classics when the homely Anglo-Saxon would serve as well.

From Babu Sarada Kanta Guha.

47, Sangattola,
Dacca, November 25, 1888.

Dear Sir,—I have to acknowledge with thanks the receipt of your kind and affectionate letter of the 21st instant. I consider it a privilege to receive communications from an important person like you. First of all, I deem it proper to confess that I am a "school boy," but it is the school boys who are generally found to be ambitious of a journalistic career, because so indifferent are our countrymen to public interests that no sooner do they begin the world than all their connection with literature, politics, &c., ceases to exist. The "Indian Nation," the "Bengalee" and other weeklies of the metropolis have their correspondents here; and on that score I asked you to appoint me your Dacca correspondent. Though a school boy myself, I have the pleasure to assure you that I am in a position to know everything that occurs in our town. I hope that my letters will all contain fresh and important events that may interest your subscribers.

You have expressed a desire always to "encourage the young." This is as it should be. Because there would be but few men to look after the young generation of India, if our true-hearted and generous countrymen (unfortunately whose number is not very large) do not care to encourage them.

I indeed cherish the ambition to be a good writer and I have made up my mind to follow in the footsteps of some recognised literary man ; hence my strong desire to read your paper.

I intended to attend Levées, Evening Parties, &c., to enable myself to give you a faithful account of His Excellency's movements here. However I have managed by some other means which I need not mention. That I have any connection with your paper is known to very few and shall not be known to many. At the pressing request of a gentleman I have sent you a letter which is too long to be published in the columns of "Reis and Rayyet." I hope you will excuse me this time; don't think that I agree with all the views of the writer thereof. It would be unbecoming on my part to indulge in a criticism of the administration of Lord Dufferin or to condemn the policy by which he was guided.

I hope you will always take a tender interest in me and favour me with kind instructions from time to time.

Yours faithfully,
SARADA KANTA GUHA.

From Mr. S. E. J. Clarke.

Bengal Chamber of Commerce,
Calcutta, December 24, 1888.

My dear Dr. Mookerjee,—I gladly pay my tribute to the courage and wisdom of your leader of today. You are a brave man who sees what is wanted in the Native Press and sets a fine example. Such an article must be productive of good, for it must lead thoughtful and India-loving natives into a better path on a higher level than most of the journalism around us.

I felt proud of *Reis and Rayyet* when I read the article.

Yours sincerely,
S. E. J. CLARKE.

From Sir Donald Mackenzie Wallace.

Government House,
Calcutta, February 16, 1889.

My dear Mookerjee,— * * *

I quite understand your old reluctance to mix much with Europeans, but now that you have to some extent come out of your shell I hope you will not crawl into it again. We greatly want men of your stamp as a connecting link and I trust that your example of manly independence may not be without effect on your countrymen. In any case, please to remember me as one of your friends though a semi-official European, and believe me,

Yours sincerely,
DONALD MACKENZIE WALLACE.

Dr. FitzEdward Hall, on his arrival in India, made the acquaintance of the well-known Dutt family of Wellington Square, whose name was a synonym for culture and hearty recognition of literary merit. Babu Rajinder Dutt was struck with his learning and ability; and introduced him to the then Bishop of Calcutta through whose influence he obtained a post in the Educational Service of the North-Western Provinces. He subsequently became Principal of the Benares College; established a reputation for sound Oriental scholarship, and, on his well-merited retirement, was appointed an examiner by the Civil Service Commissioners.

To Dr. FitzEdward Hall.

Dear Sir,—Allow me to introduce myself to you as an Oriental admirer of one of the very first of Orientalists. It is now twenty-eight years since I had the first and last opportunity of being thrown into your company. But I had known you by repute, and I am pretty familiar with your Oriental writings and have always valued them. The fact is that I am a most intimate friend of your friends the Dutts. Although a high Brahman myself, I have these thirty years regarded them and been regarded by them, to most intents and purposes, as a blood relation. Hence I early came to know or at least to know of their connections, native and European.

When you last went to see them I was summoned from my home at Baranagore in the northern suburbs, to meet you, as you had expressed a desire to see the late Kaliprosunno Singh so famous for his Bengali translation of the Mahabharata, who was a particular friend of mine. I found you in Woomesh Chunder's little room in the corner of the Baitakkhana house, as it is called, and I took you over to Jorasanko to see Singh, Woomesh's younger brother, Sooresh Chunder accompanying. You had a pretty long animated conversation with Singh which much interested and edified me.

September 17, 1889.

I wrote so far sometime ago with a faltering hand, to apprise you of the death of our common friend, Rajinder Dutt, but was interrupted and did not finish, and forgot all about it, until I received your kind note by last mail. Even then my first idea was that I had sent my letter and that yours was a reply and I actually asked Babu Jogesh Chunder Dutt (the only surviving son of the late Doorga Churn Dutt, and brother of Woomesh Chunder, Grish Chunder and Sooresh Chunder whom you knew, who besides literary assistance manages this paper, sitting at the same table with me) whether that was not so? He replied that no letter had been sent you, but only the paper. An examination of your epistle also disclosed no terms of acknowledgment of my correspondence. I have now discovered the unfinished letter.

You will have seen that we published Theodore Neal's last letter to Rajinder dated so far back as 1867 and two of May last from Mr. Silsbee to Jogesh's nephew Prakash who is at school, the latter containing references to yourself. May we make similiar use of the last letter that you wrote to the deceased?

It was very kind of Mr. Silsbee after more than thirty years to come to see Rajinder and the Dutts. He took his quarters at a neighbouring hotel and used to pass all day either at the family house down the lane or in this Baitakkhana house where I write and in which our office and press are housed. He made a great impression on us all, I myself being not the least affected. We are, whatever our faults, an affectionate people. I was deeply moved when he left us and ever after think of him from time to time, and I dare say the same is the case with others of us. If you write to him, please give him the kindest regards of "the Editor" by which title he loved to designate me.

We are all much affected by your hearty tribute to Rajinder's worth in the New York

Nation. Mr. Silsbee told me of your connection with the paper, of which he spoke highly as one of the leading organs of the country. I find it of high calibre too and should be much obliged if you could conveniently send over the copies in which your writings appear.

As you seem to have got my name in advance of my address, from the advertisement of my little book, I am bound to send you a copy, which I do with all the gratitude of expectancy. * * *

Yours most faithfully,

SAMBHU C. MOOKERJEE.

To Colonel J. C. Ardagh,

Private Secretary to the Viceroy.

Telegram, dated September 17, 1889.

Cannot the Currency Office be closed during Pooja? All Bengal will be ever grateful. Financial letter 452 of '80, Bengal 328 of '82.

To Colonel J. C. Ardagh.

September 20, 1889.

My dear Colonel Saheb,—Urged by the state

of public feeling around me among my countrymen, I have taken the liberty to send you a telegram on a public question. Under ordinary circumstances I would have written a regular letter, but the goddess is already upon us—the preliminary ceremonies have in many families begun, and if anything is to be done about the Pooja Holidays it must be done at once. The distance between Simla and the Viceroy's deserted capital in the plains is so great that I availed myself of the mighty machinery of the electric post which your own civilization had put in my hands. The matter is of the greatest importance to native society in Bengal, without distinction of creed, though, of course, it is only Hindus with rare exceptions that worship Doorga. For, irrespective of its religious connection, this Pooja is the recognized Long Vacation of the people, when men return home from great distances and all parts, when relatives and friends meet, when once in the year the exiles come not only in obedience to the dictates of kinship and affection but also to settle accounts, repair their homesteads and altogether, as the saying goes, put their houses in order. Any detraction from the integrity of such an institution cannot but be greviously felt throughout the country. If His Excellency could see his way to preserve it for the people, he might depend upon the blessings of millions.

Other rulers are gratefully remembered for their solicitude in their behalf, for the question has been settled repeatedly.

September 23.

I was writing on Friday last when I received your letter. I stopped in order to enquire whether instructions had been received at the Currency Office and what effect they would have there. I put myself in communication with the head of the Accounts Department and have learnt that a few clerks only will be required to attend, but the same men will, fairly enough, not be required to come all the days. It is calculated that more than half the Currency establishment will thus have their Doorga Pooja interfered with. This is a great pity. The effect already is that the *Indian Mirror*, in expressing the feelings of the people, foolishly talks in a style that should never be indulged in, or at any rate ought to be reserved for the last extremity. For my part, I am trying to pour oil on the troubled waters and reason my people into the belief that the evil will not prove so very great after all; that at all events Government have done as much as they could, under the circumstances, and that they ought to feel thankful to His Excellency the Viceroy.

I certainly am indebted to him for the prompt notice of my appeal, and request you will convey to His Excellency my best thanks.

Yours truly,

SAMBHU C. MOOKERJEE.

To Mr. E. F. T. Atkinson.

September 20, 1889.

My dear Atkinson,—You cannot be unaware of the strong feeling in the country on the subject of the Pooja holidays. It is a genuine feeling, due to a real grievance, and no sham product of wire-pulling patriots and publicists. It is not the political classes that are agitated but the true country and enlightened middle class of Bengali society. Had our politicals been concerned you would have heard a good deal more about it, and the smaller merchants and speculators who are behaving so ungenerously by their poor office drudges would have been astonished at the hornets' nest they had lightly disturbed.

I confess I was pained to hear that you had threatened the eighty odd clerks who had presumed to represent their grievance individually with pains and penalties unless they withdrew their respective representations. I certainly thought that you, having so long been in these Provinces, would show more sympathy with these poor helpless assistants of your great department. At any rate, they might be left without molestation to try the effect of their appeal for mercy to the generosity of higher authority.

I have no personal interest in the question. I am not and never have been in Government pay, and I have no relation or connection or friend whatever in any Government office or even mercantile firm, except perhaps a poor, very poor but most worthy friend drawing a few rupees—some Rs. 20 or Rs. 30, I believe—in a trading business. But living in the country among my people I cannot be callous to the hardships of my countrymen. The new departure has been a blow to them and they justifiably regard the policy of which it is the outcome with consternation.

I have been at the pains to appeal to the Viceroy in their behalf, and, although the time is short, I am not without hope that you may receive some communication by telegraph. If you do, I hope you will give it merciful construction. Whether, indeed, any suggestion from head-quarters come or not, I earnestly beg you will relent and do as much as now lies in your power to minish the severity of the blow and sweeten the pill.

Hoping you will appreciate the frankness of this communication,

I remain, most faithfully yours,

SAMBHU C. MOOKERJEE.

To Mr. E. F. T. Atkinson.

September 27, 1889.

My dear Mr. Atkinson—Pray excuse the delay in acknowledging, beyond the peon book, receipt of your courteous communication.

I was relieved to receive your emphatic contradiction of the rumour that had got abroad about the coercion exercised on the petitioning clerks by the Accountant General Bahadur himself. We of the press are, I confess, given to suspicion, still I had my doubts, Whatever might be your attitude on the question, I could not well believe that a great functionary in your position would so commit himself to partizanship with Keranees or against them. I told people accordingly, but thought it as well to enquire at the fountain-head.

I am glad to hear that your sympathies are with the clerks in this business, and indeed you have since given the public the best proof of it by withdrawing the obnoxious order. It seems as if you were only waiting for permission from higher authority to cancel the act of the Comptroller-General.

Your asseveration of personal sympathy with the people was hardly required, except for the suspicion to which, under trying circumstances, the best friends are liable. Sympathy comes naturally of knowledge, and your knowledge was known to me. I refer not only to your long experience of the country, but to the conversation that I had with you at your official residence, some years back, on the history and localities of Upper India. But you are one that loves to hide his light under a bushel. Such a character specially claims the regard of one who in his own way has been content to pursue his studies and do his duty by the world in obscurity, while fussy hypocrites and sciolists have been lauded to the skies and recognized as the only true men. I am, however, glad to have drawn you out, though in a confidential way, and extracted a copy of your interesting monograph on the Religions of the Himalyas. Many, many thanks for it. I will read it during the holidays and let you know. Meantime, allow me to subscribe myself, in haste,

Yours very sincerely,

SAMBHU C. MOOKERJEE.

P.S.—From the delay in your issuing the last orders on the Holidays it seems that you received a fresh communication from Simla. Was it so?

S. C. M.

From Colonel Ardagh.

Viceregal Lodge,
Simla, September 1889.

Dear Dr. Mookerjee,—I trust that the question of the Doorga Pooja Holidays upon which you have telegraphed and written to me, has, for this occasion at least, been closed to the satisfaction of those interested.

There is, however, a paragraph in your letter to me on which I wish to make a few remarks.

My telegram informed you that the Currency Offices were to be closed during the holidays with the reservation that a few clerks were to attend on certain days so that arrangements might be made for the convenience of the mercantile community. You tell me in your letter that it was calculated that the result of the order would be that "more than one half of the Currency establishment will thus have their Doorga Pooja interfered with."

I can perceive from the rest of your letter that you yourself fully appreciate the motives which actuated the Viceroy in issuing his orders upon a case which came before him unexpectedly for immediate solution, and in which it was necessary to consider and safeguard antagonistic interests ; and I am therefore somewhat surprised at your acceptance without question of an interpretation so entirely opposed to the letter and spirit of the telegram ; for it appears to me, that even by exercising the most perverse and malicious ingenuity in carrying out the order, it would still have been impossible to attain the consequences ascribed to it.

With regard to the reservation, it appeared superfluous to explain at length in the telegram that there was a possible difficulty in the way of closing altogether, dependent on certain legal obligations connected with the payment of money, which it is indispensable to guard against ; and it did not appear necessary or advisable to state that instructions had been issued that the few clerks whose presence might be needful were to be selected from those who were not Hindus, in order that none of that religion might be deprived of their holiday. In short, no greater solicitude for those concerned could possibly have been shown. I think it may be pointed out that the claim to the entire suspension of the business of the State in public departments on religious holidays of whatever creed, has never been admitted ; and a little consideration will convince you that it would be impracticable. I need only mention the Army, the Railways, and the Postal Department, in order to indicate the intolerable inconvenience which would arise from pushing such a principle to its logical conclusions. These questions must be dealt with in practice by compromises, devised in a spirit of mutual forbearance, for the general convenience of all ;—and it is to be hoped that before this question crops up again, a satisfactory arrangement may be arrived at by reasonable concessions on both sides.

I remain, yours faithfully,

J. C. ARDAGH.

To Mr. Edward Jenkins.

"Reis and Rayyet" Office,
Calcutta, October 8, 1889.

My dear Sir,—I duly received your favour of June with the valuable series of articles on the Congress. I am also receiving regularly the *Overland Mail.* I hope you get *Reis and Rayyet* by every mail, though I have yet seen no sign in your journal. I reproduced your able article on the Mahomedan Movement in connection with the Calcutta Mahomedan Literary Society. The Founder-Secretary, Nawab Abdool Luteef Bahadoor, is my intimate life-long friend. Although he is a staunch Mussalman and I am a Brahman —a Brahman of Brahmans as Dr. W. H

Russell, who had been in India, once called me—we have for thirty years been as brothers. It was a great pleasure to me to read your sympathetic views in respect of the Mahomedans with whom, alone among Hindu politicians, I have ever sympathised. That pleasure was enhanced by wonder at the freedom of your pretty long piece of writing from error of any kind such as is almost inevitable in foreign productions. Even Professor Vambéry writing to the Nawab has not been able to avoid it —he who is not only a great Orientalist but has travelled almost to the frontiers of India. One notable instance I remember. He talks of coming out to India where he hopes to address the Mahomedans in Persian, as if it were their own tongue. So far from Persian being one of the Indian vernaculars, none but learned Mussalmans of the old class know it, and few of those who have read Persian can speak it or understand it when spoken. The Professor might just as well address an Indian

Mahomedan audience in Hungarian! Lord Dufferin committed the same mistake. He told me that he learnt Persian because he was informed that it was the *lingua franca* of Asia and he hoped to be able to communicate direct with the people. But he found to his disappointment that not even the best of Mahomedans understood him or could converse in Persian. The Hindustani has better claims to be regarded as a sort of *lingua franca*, but even that is not generally understood as people are apt to imagine.

Why don't you collect your articles on the Indian Congress and the reform of the Legislative Councils? They quite merit separate publication in a permanent form. I have myself from the first been of opinion that the movement set on foot by Mr. Allan Hume and his native followers—some of them men of great accomplishments and ability and, what is better, of real patriotism, however misguided—

was premature. And of course I am the butt of their abuse and ill will. They will find out their mistake when they succeed in obtaining any large measure of representation by election. Already, we don't find men for our municipal boards. How will they fill a Chamber of Deputies?

Allow me to send for your kind acceptance a copy of a small book of travels at home. * * *

My book has not been published in England. It bears no Indian publishers' name even, being issued from this office. Nor is it for sale at any booksellers' in this country or in any other. I need scarcely say how thankful I shall be to have any suggestions or corrections from so famous a master of the craft.

I remain,
My dear Sir,
Most truly yours,
SAMBHU C. MOOKERJEE.

To Mr. G. Syamala Row.

October 8, 1889.

My dear Mr. Syamala Row,—You have knocked at an auspicious season and, indeed, on the very Day of Luck. This is the evening of the full moon (after the Dusserah) on which the Goddess of Fortune, Lakshmi is worshipped. We are in the chronological centre of our Doorga Pooja Long Vacation. The whole weekly journalism of Bengal Proper is in abeyance. There is still work enough for me at any rate,—more than ever perhaps but it is not of an exigent kind. Your first letter missed fire by coming at an unfortunate moment. The fact is, I did not see it in time; but months after I picked up an open letter which was yours. It is difficult—I may at once say impossible to attend to all the letters received by an editor. But it is not the young or the obscure that are neglected in this office. I am at once a bad and good correspondent:

I am irregular and forgetful, but when I do write I pour out my mind, writing at length and conversing on paper. I am afraid I bore my correspondents, as at this moment, with my long-windedness. I am unfortunately a prey to a monologous and discursive habit. I love to encourage the young, and so they are pretty sure of hearing from me, however much I may offend exalted personages. Just now I might be addressing more than one noble Lord both here and in England, but I prefer Mr. G. V. Syamala Row.

So far so good. And now for the bad. For business, you know, is business—usually a hard, dry, disagreeable thing—at best a miserable yarn.

I truly regret that I cannot give you an answer after your heart. Your productions so far as I have read the pieces forwarded, are not poetry. They are not good verse, either ; sometimes no verse at all. For all that, you may find many openings for publication in the Native Press. Indeed, some of the pieces—the Lines to Allan Hume and the Greeting to Norton and Bonnerjee, have already appeared in the *Hindu*—so much the worse for that excellent paper! I am sorry that my brother editors do not know better. It is evidence of that want of culture and of that absence of the critical faculty that degrades our press in the opinion of European society. The truth unfortunately is that with the exception of two Parsis, Mr. Padshah of Calcutta and Mr. Malabari of Bombay, our journalists are singularly deficient in literature. Even the Anglo-Indian Press is weak to a degree in this respect, as was confessed last year when the editor of a leading Calcutta daily sent over to this Press Mr. Locke Richardson, the Shakespearean reciter, with a note of introduction to me, to be examined in his pretensions. It is passing strange that the experienced editors of the *Hindu*, who are unquestionably clever and able men, do not see the utter inanity, the halting verbosity, and the defective construction of such a piece as your Greeting fond to "magnificent seditionists." These faults are so glaring that you yourself ought to see them. You have evidently not matter and language enough for heroics. Accordingly, the gaps are mechanically filled up with expletives and useless epithets, and you are reduced to frequent repetition and idle interrogation. The same difficulty, for the same reason, you experience with your stanzas. Take the first: It is one mass of repetition of a single salutation—"Hail, Norton and Bonnerjee!" For these four words you have employed twenty. You were met by a difficulty at the outset—to make up eight syllables of your first line. So you called your "mild Hindu" "meek"—which certainly does not advance the matter. The stanza is open to a more serious objection.

It causes a "derangement of epitaphs." There is no knowing Who's is who? An English reader would take Norton to be the mild Hindu, and Bonnerjee to be England's worthy child. So you see that, notwithstanding your lavish expenditure of words, you have not made your ordinary opening salutation clear and have confused the identity of its objects. The second stanza opens promisingly, but the promise is broken before reaching the semicolon. From "A nation's gratitude and love" what a fall is "in this place!"—a perfectly irrelevant phrase whose impertinence you suffer meekly, nay, actually invite, in order to secure the benefit of the answering rhyme. Well for you could you keep clear of both *place* and *race!* But for these, perhaps, you might escape the lamentable sinking of your verse. You might then possibly avoid such an awkward sentiment—"Naught can our thankfulness remove." Then you could not possibly write "we are a grateful race." I wonder you do not see the solemn ridiculousness of that dictum in the connection. All your rhymes are of the same character, not flowing naturally from the thought, but commanding it.

You have matter, such as it is, for no more than a couple of stanzas, at most three. This you spread out into eight. Vigorous writing in prose and metre is out of the question under such circumstances. You have either a defective notion of metrical diction, or, in striving to make bricks without straw, you suppress your critical sense for the nonce. The latter is, of course, the true theory, and you unnecessarily reduce me to remind you that "in this place," "returning here," and such like words and phrases can only sink the fair bark of Lyric Poesy. Besides the tautology, the opening line is marred by the adjective "-able," a word which has no business in verse. Shall I tell you that the only decent thing in your Greeting—at any rate in your eight stanzas—is a single adjective—"peerless." "Peerless Norton" is excellent. The whole line is very good, "Our peerless Norton come!" and the best of the eight lines.

So there is yet hope for you, if you give your higher self play and be in no hurry to be a famous poet before you have gone through the necessary discipline—of which this letter may well be regarded as a part—and acquired the requisite fund of observation and ideas. This latter is a question of time, except for a few favoured souls who seem to descend on our earth fully equipped.

But how came you to write such stuff as the opening lines of your heroic couplets?

"All hail to you, my country's faithful friends,
From Britain's isle, on which our ideal depends,
And where you worked so well for Bharat-land,
That we can, sure, achieve a success grand."

The very punctuation, carefully as you

have, in obedience to metrical necessity, punctuated the passage, is faulty. There is not, in an opening salutation, a single mark of admiration, either at the beginning, in the middle, or at the end. The grammar is not better in other respects. What does "And" connect? It is a mere stop-gap. "Can" ought to be "might." There is no end to the filling-in process. What a succession of pleonasms in "Britain's isle" and "Bharat-land!" Say you that it is Bharat—and not Bhárat? Does that mend the matter? Do you ordinarily say—Johnson-land or Goldsmith-land? Why not say at once *Bharat's land?* Of course, without special warning, most readers will read "Bharat-land" as if it were *Bhárat-land.* The crowning blunder is in the scanning of the last line. Are our brethren in the South accustomed to pronounce the penultimate word as *suc-cess?* Or, how came the *Hindu* to admit such a verse?

Your ballad is better, because therein you have something like a story to tell and that form is more easy to imitate. But do, like a good boy, eschew all attempts at blank verse. You can produce only bad and queer prose in the effort to write poetry. Even Southey and Wordsworth are frequently prosaic to the last degree.

The sonnet is not only a difficult but also a delicate business, which has been beyond many true poets and men of genius. You ought to have recognised the fact in the instance you quote. Boccage's sonnet may be good in the Portuguese, but what a poor thing in the English version! It is well written, and, I dare say, faithful enough. Your imitation is good, perhaps better. But what, after all, is there in it?

October 9.

An imitation cannot substantially go beyond the original. What is there in the original, I ask? Nelson comes bleeding from the field of battle to Elysium, makes an indifferent, not to say foolish, speech to the poor affrighted ghosts, bragging of having raised Europe from thraldom, a pretence finally reduced by the speaker himself to his having thrown a bolt against France for which his own countrymen were mighty glad and thankful to him ; then Alexander, the Macedonian military lunatic, after his juvenile habit, weeps and envies the new comer, although the latter had defeated only one nation on the seas. Such is the substance ; nor is it set out by drapery and accessories. It is quite possible that Boccage's Portuguese is good, even fine, but the English rendering is not so. All the spirit and spirituality have evaporated in the process of transferring literature from one tongue to another. The truth is, translation is an impossibility. It is usually a sort of literary murder. * * *

Your friend, I dare say, is a clever, even a brilliant young man, and I shall be glad to hear of him and from him if he likes it. But you pay *Reis and Rayyet* a poor compliment by stating so confidently that his ballad deserves a place in its columns. Indeed, you seem, in the fervour of a youthful friendship, to have conceived an exaggerated opinion of its excellence. In point of fact, it is not so very distinctly or specifically above the level of your own compositions in manuscript that you send me. If you wish to see what brilliant university men and medallists can do, take up the Cambridge Prize Poems. But, for a foreigner, your friend's piece and, indeed, your own ones not in print are creditable. His "Dufferin" is a trifle superior, perhaps, in neatness, being short, but it is essentially of the same class with yours. Both are effusions of not only unfledged poets but also juvenile politicians. It is strange the unreality of your productions and the absurdity of the ideas did not strike you. It is possible to dislike Lord Dufferin and avoid these faults.

But why still "rub it into" the poor Marquis of Dufferin and Ava? Is he never to be forgiven for having saved an empire stranded by his predecessor? Why, your very leaders, who started the dead set against him, are themselves ashamed of their injustice. In fact, the word has been passed, to praise Lord Dufferin as a seasoned, masterful and sagacious statesman, without bias, and to fight for the reforms he recommended. Your friend sings:—

> "He found the Rishis' sacred land
> United all in love,
> The Turk and Brahman, hand in hand,
> With blessing from above."

That may be poetry. But is it truth? Was the Rishis' land even so very united? Then how did it cease to be the Rishis' land to become the Mlechhas' dependency?

If by the blessing of God, the Turk or Mussalman and Brahman were in any sense "hand in hand" in these latter days, was it Lord Dufferin that "set them by the ears," or was it your own dear Ripon? Was it not rather that Lord Dufferin did his best to heal the differences caused by the stupid and weak bungling of his predecessor and succeeded? Surely, the cultivation of poetry does not absolve us from the obligation of justice. Justice is due to the D—l. Is Dufferin alone to go without it?

After all, your and your friend's verses have considerable merit as exercises, if not sufficient for public acceptance. You must not suffer yourselves to be discouraged. You have everything for success except age and experience, and these are bound to come—they are already upon you, hastening to greet you as I write. You both are remarkably clever young men. I wish we had some such products of our Calcutta University. I am astonished at your command of English. Your letter under reply would not be disowned by many educated Englishmen. Poetry is an exceptional product, and some of the greatest men have failed in it. I would not say one word to dissuade you from the practice of verse. It will go off without anybody's interference, or you will burst upon the world as a true singer. Meanwhile, I would ask you to write prose as well, as much as you can. There is a poetry in prose too—a rhythm and melody as well as a passion and sentiment akin to those of the masters of song. But I would not have you attempt that even. If it come naturally you will not be able to help it. Write naturally and straightforwardly, whether in prose or verse—with honest manliness, using your own thoughts and your own language, without trying to write after somebody else. However, all this is superfluous advice. You have already acquired a singular facility in writing English.

I wish I could ask you to eschew politics. But this is impossible. You cannot even keep clear of the degrading local and party politics of the day. At all events, try to make them secondary to higher studies—Jurisprudence and the Science of Government and History.

Need I ask your pardon for this long despatch and its severity ? I address a surprizing intelligence, and I hope my letter justifies itself. I love you and your friend as my country's hope. I love you in special for your connection with Appa Row. I could not give you better proof than the trouble I have taken in appraising your work and the trouble I am taking in giving judgment.

You scarcely deserve such consideration. See how scurvily your other Row treated me ! After having roused in me the greatest interest and even affection, he gave me up without notice. For long I was in great anxiety about his fate. I was glad to learn from your first letter that he has settled down to a profession. God bless him ! Does he continue his addresses to the Muses ? He has the stuff in him.

Your sincere friend and well-wisher,

SAMBHU C. MOOKERJEE.

P.S.—Your "Tantia" is interesting and will appear on the 26th.

S. C. M.

The succeeding letter was written by the veteran editor of the *Statesman* when racked with ill-health which he sought in vain to alleviate by a visit to Darjeeling. Mr. Knight's allusion to "Tippera" refers to the arrears of salary as paid adviser, which are mentioned at page 44 of the memoir. It is much to be wished that the Durbar may acknowledge the services of their old and faithful servant by paying his widow a portion at least of these long due arrears.

From Mr. R. Knight.

Darjeeling, October 25, 1889.

Dear Mookerjee,—It was most kind of you to send me that letter from Barakhar, and although I can not reply to it, accept the will for the deed, and my grateful acknowledgments for remembering how gladly I should hear from you. It is very distressing to me to hear that pecuniary anxiety of any kind is burdening you. You do not tell me whether the Maharaja of Tippera made any response to my appeal to him to liquidate your claims? If he does not reply, I shall write sharply to him on the subject when I hear from you again. Your description of the Fornaro Bungalow amused and interested me greatly. May God generously restore your health, and enable you to continue the "Reis and Rayyet" with the extraordinary literary ability and moral force that distinguish its columns! I look upon you as a sort of "ballast" in the ship in which new India is embarked, and the need there is of this moderating and steadying force is conspicuous enough; but upon the whole I wonder greatly at the strides that young India are making and feel that it is the native press that will erelong be the controlling force in the country. * *

Yours very sincerely,

R. KNIGHT.

From Lord Stanley of Alderley.

October 31, 1889.

Dear Mr. Mookerjee,—A short time ago I received a copy of the "Empress" of Calcutta, for which I suppose I have to thank you, as it contained a portrait of yourself and a biographical sketch: the latter was what I expected and might have written myself, but the portrait was quite different from the idea I had formed of you, for I had not heard any description of you. I am glad to see you in those Oriental garments, for I should not have thought you had worn such since you left Tippera, and they must be inconvenient amongst the "Reis and Rayyet" printing presses.

* * *

To Dr. FitzEdward Hall.

November 26, 1889.

Dear Sir,—I am in receipt of your letter of the 18th October. Coming from a veteran Pandit, it is one to be thankful for, but being an answer it hardly leaves room for excuse for boring you again. I should, however, like to put in just a word. You are not right in supposing that I have little interest for questions in English philology. I take great interest in them. One of the points that drew me to you is my respect for you as one entitled to authority in that department of learning. As a reader of the journal of the Asiatic Society of Bengal I noticed your speciality long since. Some of your foot notes to your contributions appeared to me most interesting and your criticisms therein showed knowledge as well as acuteness. Formerly, when Dr. Rajendralala Mitra was a simple scholar and we were friends (he was a contributor to my *Mookerjee's Magazine*, now defunct, and I revised the first volume of his *Orissa*), meeting almost every evening, I used to tease him by referring to your handling of his writings. A haughty, disdainful man, he could never bear my speaking of you as the most accurate

Sanskritist since the death of Colebrooke, who had read more Sanskrit books and MSS. than any other scholar, American, British or Continental, and had a more critical knowledge of the English language into the bargain. But he never could say anything to alter my judgment, always contenting himself with alleging your comparative ill success in the literary world. Of course, I omit the expressions of mere personal vexation with which he embellished his conversation about you. Perhaps I am not right in reporting this even in the confidence of a private correspondence. For, though we have long ceased to be on speaking terms, I would not do anything dishonourable to even my worst enemy. I mention the matter to show that I have long been familiar with you and your writings, though unknown to you personally. I have since followed your career as far as I have been able according to my opportunities. I have never been able to see your book on

English, but I read your article in the *Nineteenth Century.* I am not strong in Old English, because the researches into the subject were started after I left College, and I have not had time to take it up since. Our Principal, Captain Richardson, (whom you may remember as the "D. L. R." of Anglo-Indian Literature) was well versed in the language from Chaucer and Gower downwards, and he was a great critic of the old Jeffrey, Hazlitt and Leigh Hunt school. I have devoted myself with passionate fondness to your literature and have marked the successive changes in the language since it has had a literature properly speaking. If you ever write anything which you think might interest me—now I have acquainted you with my turn—I shall be much obliged by your putting me in the way of reading it, at least by giving me the reference. I once thought of communicating some gleanings from my note books to Dr. Murray for the new Dictionary. But I had so many distractions that I did not carry out my intention. The thing is, I pursue too many studies and have no concentration. Otherwise, perhaps, I might have made some mark. I see inferior men who know much less do it.

Yours most truly,
SAMBHU C. MOOKERJEE.

To Professor A. Vambéry.

Buda Pest University, Buda Pest, Austria.

December 10, 1889.

Honoured Professor,—I am an Oriental and so are you—by personal sympathy and primitive origin. Although you have travelled far in Asia you have not yet been far enough in this direction to reach these shores. Your Eastern peregrinations and experiences have been confined to the lands and peoples of Islam. Yet I feel confident that you cannot but feel kindly to the other countries and races of this vast continent—the original home of your own ancient ancestry. Though a Hindu myself, indeed a Brahman of Brahmans, I have always watched your career with interest and admiration. Perhaps, I am an exceptional person who has always loved the Mahomedans as brethren and has earnestly tried to interpret between Hindus and Mahomedans and effect a union of hearts between two peoples whose social and political interests in India are identical. This *rôle* of go-between has come natural to me from my intimate association with Mahomedans and my knowledge of them and their literature and history. It is with a sense of personal pain that I have viewed how the influence of English prejudice against those from whom the British wrested the government of the country and of the education given by them to the people here, was creating an estrangement between the two most important elements in the population. There has of late been a reaction among the British so far as to make them look kindly upon the Mahomedans as a possible support of their power against the pretensions of the Hindus, the tall talk of whose leaders, trained by European instruction, has caused them alarm. But then, unfortunately, they are trying, in their fancied immediate object, to sow dissensions between the two bodies. My ideal is to form a nation by a harmonious social fusion of the two component parts of the population under the British Crown, which has given us such a strong and equitable Government as we could never hope to form ourselves; which has advanced us to a new life, and is daily improving us, and which I devoutly pray will keep us in hand until the time comes under God's Providence when we are in a position to help ourselves.

Pardon this egotistic rigmarole. It is necessary to give you an idea of intersectional politics in British India and of my relation to them as a condition *sine qua non* of any useful or intelligible correspondence.

Your letter to my friend Nawab Abdool Luteef Bahadoor of the 12th August appeared in most of the Indian papers and was commented upon in many. I devoted a leading article to it in my issue of the 7th September and directed a copy to be sent to you. At the Nawab's instance the article with your letter was reprinted in a separate sheet for circulation. I took the opportunity to make some slight corrections, which I hope improved the thing. I dare say you received some copies from the Nawab direct.

On the 10th November I published an article on "The Sultan and his Views on the Eastern Question" in which I made the account of your interview with His Majesty which appeared in a Pesth newspaper my text. I have since been troubled by seeing a Mahomedan from Constantinople giving in a London journal a dismal report of the state of matters at the Turkish capital. According to him, the Sultan is a weak-brained man now on the verge of madness, freakish, taking counsel of menials, interfering in the minutest details of administration, and changing his ministers on frivolous pretexts, while his shelved brother has recovered his health and wits and is ready to resume office and power, with the concurrence of the *Ulema* and the Pashas. That goes counter to your testimony, as I read it. What is the truth? or what the explanation?

Yours faithfully,
SAMBHU C. MOOKERJEE.

From Professor A. Vambéry.

Budapest University,
Budapest, December 31, 1889.

Dear Sir,—I have received your letter dated December the 10th with great interest, having had the pleasure in finding in your views and intentions the experimental solution of a question which has long time engaged my full attention. In presenting yourself as "an exceptional person who has always loved the Mahomedans as brethren and has earnestly tried to interpret between Hindus and Mahomedans and effect a union of hearts between two peoples whose social and political interests in India are identical," you have certainly put before yourself a very useful, but at the same time a very arduous task. As far as my limited experience and unpretentious notions go, the solution of this problem in Asia has always seemed to me an unanswerable difficulty. You evidently know better than myself, that in Asia the partition wall between mankind is not the nationality, but religion. The Mahomedan scripture says—"All true believers are brethren," as well as that unbelievers are one nation, a saying which implies a strict unity between the followers of one faith, and does not admit any partition by race or nationality. I am, therefore, at a loss to understand how your idea to form a nation by a harmonious social fusion of the two component parts of the population, sublime and high-minded as that idea is, could be carried out without shaking the very foundation of the respective communities. Of course you are on the best way in proposing to effect that idea "under the British Crown, which has given us such a strong and equitable Government as we could never hope to form ourselves; which has advanced us to a new life, and is daily improving us, and which I devoutly pray will keep us in hand until the time comes under God's Providence when we are in a position to help ourselves." This argument speaks decidedly whole volumes in favour of the soundness of your views. The time will and must come when many of your countrymen and co-religionists will share in these healthy views, but I beg leave to say that this time is yet very, very far and that it would be much easier to make all Europe one community of a common interest and aim, than to mould the different nationalities and creeds of Hindustan into one nation. What you have to do is to proceed on the way inaugurated by your British teachers without any premature aspirations unfit and eventually dangerous to the present stage of culture of the great mass of the peoples of India. What you have achieved hitherto under the guidance of Great Britain and assisted by the innate splendid mental capacities of your people, is quite unique in the history of civilization of mankind. Your hitherto made progress appears the best guarantee for the future development of India. You enjoy liberties which are the object of envy not only of all Asia and Russia, but also of many parts of Europe, and the benignant rays of liberty will certainly increase in the measure as the sun of enlightenment rises over the horizon of your vast and glorious country.

This is the humble advice I can give you, as one who is not influenced by political, national, or religious interests, but who, bearing the welfare and prosperity of poor Asia at heart, has always felt happy on seeing down-trodden mankind raised to a better future.

As to your question about the discrepancy between my statements in reference to the character of Sultan Abdul Hamid and those of a Mahomedan correspondent in the *Daily News*, I beg leave to say that the writer in the last-named paper is not a Turk but evidently an Ottoman subject living in London and discontented with the rule of the Sultan—and further I beg leave to call to your memory the fact that the said newspaper is the mouthpiece of a political party in England shortsighted enough to declare open war against 50 millions of their fellow citizens and ready to find fault with the Ottomans whom they have styled the unspeakable Turk worthy to be driven bag and baggage out of Europe. Whilst my experience of the character of the present ruler of Turkey is taken from a personal intercourse with the

Sultan and from a long-standing connection with the leading men on the Bosphorus. The difference of means and modes of observation must naturally entail different results.

Thanking you for your suggestive letter and sending my kindest regards to Nawab Abdool Luteef Bahadur, I beg to remain,

Yours faithfully,

A. VAMBERY.

A *Gazette of India* Extraordinary, giving the programme of reception, on the 3rd January 1890, between 3-30 and 4-30 P.M., at Prinsep's Ghat, Calcutta, of H. R. H. Prince Albert Victor of Wales, was published on the 30th December 1889. According to the programme, only the Maharaja of Kuch Behar, the Nawab Bahadur of Murshidabad, and Maharaja Jotendro Mohun Tagore were to be presented to His Royal Highness at the Ghat. Their exclusion was naturally resented by the Chiefs from Behar and other provinces who had come to Calcutta to do the Prince honour. Attempts were made to have the omission rectified. When they failed, Dr. Mookerjee was asked to intercede. On the 2nd January he wrote to the Private Secretary to the then Viceroy and received a reply which was balm to the wounded dignity of the Chiefs.

To Col. J. C. Ardagh.

January 2, 1890.

My dear Colonel Saheb,—Allow me to offer you and your noble Chief my cordial and loyal wishes for a happy New Year and a comfortable and pleasant residence and bright and beneficent career in the East.

After compliments, business. I was unwell the last two days, or I might have disturbed you in the midst of the festivities for bidding adieu to the Old Year and welcoming the New. Having recovered, I hasten to perform my duty of apprising you of the dissatisfaction caused by the arrangements announced for to-morrow's reception of the Prince. I refer to the provision for three

Indian magnates only being presented to His Royal Highness at the landing. This is regarded as a slight, not to say insult, to the great Chiefs present in town, some of whom have come at no small sacrifice on purpose to do honour to the Prince. Notwithstanding that His Royal Highness is on a private visit, their sense of duty to one so near to the Throne and so dear to Her Majesty the Empress would not allow them to stay at home, enjoying ease, attending to their own business and saving money. Their presence and their expenditure in honour of the Prince are particularly welcome and will go far to save the credit of the country after the collapse of the public meeting. The Maharaja of Vizianagram went down to Madras where he gave munificently towards the reception and then hurried up to Calcutta where he has been equally liberal. The Maharaja of Durbhanga telegraphed that he would bear the whole cost and followed himself to take part in the ceremonies in person. The Chiefs of Dumraon and Bettia too are here for the purpose. You may well imagine in what a false position they find themselves by being thus pointedly ignored after all.

I do not mention the Tippera Prince, for whom I may be supposed to have a partiality. But there are others of lesser note here who are all ambitious of recognition on the occasion. There is no legitimate ground of complaint in their behalf, perhaps. But the principal Chiefs stand on a different and unique footing and they are not accustomed to be ignored. Their grievance is accentuated by the preference shown to a Bengali gentleman of Calcutta who, whatever his personal worth or wealth, was a simple Babu a few years ago, and has no influence, not to say prestige, in the country. The Nawabs of Dacca have an equal claim with him. Burdwan, a far superior one.

Durbhanga, Dumraon and Bettia are not

ordinary Zemindars, distinguished only for wealth or the extent of their estates. They are genuine territorial Chiefs and political factors. Above all, Vizianagram is a historic name and almost a sovereign Prince.

I do not know Bettia or Dumraon. I have not seen either Vizianagram or Durbhanga on the subject of the publication of the notification. But I know how these are regarded by them and I am hearing the comments of those who understand them.

Hereafter, at all events, you are sure to hear a good deal. I trust the matter will be carefully considered, and I hope it is not too late to do justice to deserving claims.

Yours most faithfully,
SAMBHU C. MOOKERJEE.

From Colonel J. C. Ardagh.

Government House,
Calcutta, January 2, 1890.

Dear Dr. Mookerjee,—Many thanks for your good wishes which I heartily reciprocate.

As regards the principal subject of your letter, I am happily able to give you reassuring information. When the programme was first made out, it was not either necessary or possible to be specific and it was simply laid down that territorial Chiefs, great families and official representatives should at least constitute a portion of the magnates who should be presented to the Prince.

Typical names were given, *e.g.*, Kuch Behar and Murshidabad, and an idea seems to have spread abroad that those alone were to be presented. This, however, I am assured, is quite erroneous. I do not at this moment possess any official list of the names, but from memory I can confidently say that I recollect the names of Durbhanga, Bettia, Dumraon, Vizinagram and Gidhour, and that there were many besides.

It would, of course, be necessary to draw the line somewhere, and it might not be very easy to draw it; but I trust it will be found that as many as reasonably could be put in this list, have been so provided for, and that the apprehensions you express will prove groundless. I should regret exceedingly any arrangement such as you hinted at, and I felt that there must have been a misunderstanding, and that the omission of the Chiefs was never contemplated.

I write in haste, but hope I have reassured you.

Yours very truly,

J. C. ARDAGH.

To Colonel J. C. Ardagh.

January 3, 1890.

My dear Colonel Saheb,—It was a great pleasure to receive your reply of last evening. The personages immediately concerned were doubtless much relieved at the final liberality of today's programme. * * *

Yours very truly,

SAMBHU C. MOOKERJEE.

From Sardar Atar Singh, Chief of Bhadaur.

Bhadaur House,

Ludhiana, January 31, 1890.

My dear Babu Saheb,—It is with regret and anxiety that I learnt from my official, who was lately at Calcutta and who twice tried to wait on you before his leaving Calcutta, of the illness of yourself. I, however, trust that you may have recovered your health before long, and therefore beg to be informed at your earliest convenience of the state of your health. Praying for your perfect recovery and continual good health, with long life, for the good of the country, I remain,

Yours sincerely,

ATAR SINGH.

From Dr. Makendralal Sircar.

51, Sankaritola,

Calcutta, March 18, 1890.

My dear Sambhu,—I do not deserve half of what you have written to Mr. Routledge. What I did for you, what I always do for you, is out of the purest affection never alloyed with the remotest thought of any other remuneration than that of a return of the same affection. Believe me, when I say that your life is no less precious to me than my own. For the preservation of that life, I am prepared to do what is in my power to do.

Now, my dear Sambhu, if you have a real affection for me, as I fully believe you have, I must ask you to help forward with your powerful pen the cause of the dearest object of my life. If I mistake not, in the matter of science cultivation by our countrymen, you entertain the same strong views that I do. And, therefore, it would be no partiality to an old friend if you plead on behalf of the only Institution in all India which has inaugurated real, independent, natural, scientific education, the permanency of which means the regeneration of this degenerate country.

With the sincerest love, ever yours,

MAHENDRALAL SIRCAR.

To Mr. James Routledge.

March 18, 1890.

My dear Friend,—You will be delighted to have a line from my own hand I know, after the great illness through which I have passed. I, therefore, hasten to write to you before I commence correspondence with my friends in India. It was a severe visitation—the inflammation of both lungs all over, at my time of life, in a man of sedentary habits and a broken-down constitution. But God the Great Healer granted me a fraternal physician of the highest skill and tact in Dr. Sircar, and He also gave me the prudence and patience to submit myself entirely to him. He came several times in the 24 hours every day, watched at my bed side and did the needful, though himself in indifferent health and having fifty things to attend to besides his practice. And all this without any hope of remuneration. Nor am I a solitary object of his professional benevolence.

His house is a hospital for the relief of out-door patients, hundreds of whom besiege it daily. And neighbours and friends he visits at their houses free. Are there many such doctors in England, glorious in many respects, moral as well as material, and famous for organized charity? I am afraid the struggle for life is far too keen there to encourage this sort of patriarchal benevolence. My illness has been a very protracted business. Although I sat up in bed soon enough, I was literally confined there for two months. You must have observed for some weeks past traces of my pen in *Reis and Rayyet.* Before that I could give instructions by word of mouth as to one or two leading topics. I am very sorry that I was myself passing through the crisis of my disease when the life of not only one of the truest friends of India and humanity, but also a rare man of refined delicacy and overflowing goodness closed within almost a stone's throw of me, so that I was not able to do the last offices of friendship towards Robert Knight. I could not even write the notice obituary, though I could, and that with difficulty, supply the particulars of his life and my impressions to my excellent friend and disciple Mr. Saroda Prasad Banerjee, a private school-master, who as well my friend and assistant Mr. Jogesh Chunder Dutt, (the same who informed you and other friends of my illness,) are conducting the paper. Knight and I differed on many questions of home and foreign or outside politics. He was a man of strong likes and dislikes. I cultivate only loves and harbour no hates. Though enthusiastic to a degree by temperament, it was a calm philosophical ardour subordinated to reason and justice. He could not bear the Mussulmans. I have been trying all my life to make the two sects like each other so as to weld them together into a nation. I have a partiality for the Turks in Europe, the more from the injustice done them by the nations of Christendom since the Osmanli ceased to be a conquering Power. He would " chuck " them into the Bosphorus. I am against the dismemberment of the British Empire. I cannot bear the thought of the separation of the distant Australasian Colonies. How much must I be opposed to the cutting away of a vital member like Ireland, you may imagine. And so on. For all that, we loved each other with the highest esteem. Hundreds, if not thousands, of letters passed between us. He asked my opinion on every difficulty, political or personal. His was the only European table at which I have sat with the family as one of them. Friendship got the better of my Brahmanic prudence.

Many thanks for your communications to *Reis and Rayyet.* The more the merrier! I have a great horror of vivisection and consider all cruelty to animals cowardly. I was out the first time since my illness on Friday last at Government House to see the Viceroy, who received me most kindly, enquiring sympathetically about my illness. I asked the Private Secretary whether the subject of vivisection was before the Government of India. Not that he knew of, said he, beyond the Cruelty to Animals Bill before the Viceroy's Council.

Yours affectionately,

SAMBHU C. MOOKERJEE.

P.S.—We have not seen the Hyderabad Commission Report. It has not appeared in India.

S. C. M.

To Mr. Paul Knight.

March 20, 1890.

Dear Paul,—I am not yet out of the Doctor's hands and am still on hospital diet and condemned all night and day to the Arctic Voyager's woollens without the alleviation of a bath, but for all that I am tolerably well and have long since been out of danger. I have often proposed to write to you or your mother, but have shrunk from the effort as too much for my feeble health. I have not yet commenced to write to friends, and the few notes I have issued have been under some unavoidable necessity. This one too I would rather have avoided.

For, how can I approach you? What words can I find suitable for sympathy in your unparalleled bereavement? It is not only the death of a tender parent—it is the loss of a patriarch

> "Who loved his charge but never loved to lead,
> One whose meek flock his people loved to be,
> Not lured by any cheat of birth
> But by his clear-grained human worth
> And brave old wisdom of sincerity!"

You lived for Englishmen a unique life, parents and children and grown up sons. Sons in the same place and same household, working at the same business, and eating at the same board, all united in the bonds of the love of kinsmen and of the mutual and common interest of partners. Your calamity is far greater than the loss of an ordinary loving father, even a bread-winning father. But there is no help for the dispensations of Providence and God himself gives us the strength to bear his visitations. You must now cheer up for your mother's sake who has lost husband of whom any Queen might be proud.

If you have lost your father and your mother her lord, I have lost one of the dearest and best friends I ever possessed. I need not say more. If you have ever had a friend you may understand what that loss means. I never could believe that he was so seriously ill. When he passed away I was unconscious, myself under the shadow of Death. It will ever be a painful recollection that I could not perform the last offices of friendship.

* * *

Pray convey my sympathy to all your brothers and sisters and Mr. Harrington, and tender my respectful condolence to your good mother, and believe me to be, my dear Paul,

Yours most sincerely,
SAMBHU C. MOOKERJEE.

To Mr. J. Wood-Mason.

April 5, 1890.

My dear Wood-Mason,—There is some anxiety in the native town in consequence of the prevalence of small-pox, influenza and cholera. Our wise men are particularly exercised since they have discovered the small-pox germ in the vegetable kingdom itself! There is no use in laughing. Small-pox in plants may be one of the many things India has to teach Europe. It is admitted that the superior knowledge of Asia saved Europe from the ravages of the small-pox.

There is certainly an eruption in the Neem tree Azadirachta Indica (Azadirachta, Roxburgh's *Flora Indica*) whose leaves and flowers

I send you. I would put a leaf with well-marked spots under the microscope.

Will you ask Dr. King also?

Yours sincerely,

SAMBHU C. MOOKERJEE.

To the Marquis of Dufferin and Ava.

British Embassy, Rome.

1, Uckoor Dutt's Lane,
Calcutta, April 22, 1890.

My dear Lord,—I hope you do not start at this familiarity. With the emancipation of your individuality from the associations of the wielder of imperial authority over a sixth of the human race, you must be prepared for some indications of freedom—occasional out-breaks of human nature. No longer the formidable White Mogul of all India, you may be loved without high treason or low suspicion. Nor is there any risk from such regards. The most gushing sentiment from the antipodes cannot be very dangerous.

I have long wished to write, but you had

had enough of India, and meanwhile other things and beings claimed your Lordship's attention—your private affairs and personal friends, no less than business of State—and it seemed almost cruel at such a period to inflict on you twaddle from the banks of the Ganges. India, indeed, you were scarcely permitted to forget altogether for even a day. For a most enviable welcome awaited you at home. Your countrymen received your Lordship in triumph in recognition of your success in the East. Your eloquent allusions to your Indian career came to us flying on the wings of the post. I hope you are now more composed and in some leisure to your humble acquaintance in the far distance.

My present writing is due to a natural impulse to communicate with friends far and near on recovery from an illness which had nearly proved fatal. I was laid prostrate with double pneumonia, caught from exposure on the evening of the entertainment given by Bengal to His Royal Highness Prince Albert Victor. At my time of life, with a weak chest inherited from my maternal side, it was a serious affair. From inflammation, destruction of the substance of both lungs set in, and the doctors were alarmed. Luckily, I had in my dear old friend Dr. Sircar (whom you may remember as a member of the Bengal Legislature and Founder-Honorary Secretary of the Science Association) a most distinguished physician on whom I entirely relied, and by a course of patient watching and careful treatment he succeeded in bringing me round. Of course, the Great Healer is God Almighty and He has been pleased to spare me.

My friends and a part of the public too showed great concern on the occasion. The Nawab Bahadur of Murshidabad sent his brother and his Secretary, * *

* * *

The Viceroy's Private Secretary sent to enquire and Lord Lansdowne himself told me that he had been enquiring about my health of Dr. Sircar. The first day I ventured out I called at Government House before they left for Simla, and both Private Secretary and Principal were most kind. His Lordship was particularly busy that day, but Colonel Ardagh being called suddenly up from the animated conversation we were having on the Native States to the Viceroy's room, and happening to mention that I was with him, he was told to send me up. His Lordship not only received me cordially and made the kindest enquiries, but, what was more to my purpose, on my telling him that that morning's stethoscope examination had still disclosed a slight rawness of surface in the back, said it was nothing, that medical scrutiny always detected something wrong in some organ or other of the best of us, and by mentioning the cases of his friends, (one of whom, Lord Jervis, visited him in India that very season) really succeeded in dispelling my anxieties. I considered myself really lucky in having seen his Lordship. Then he led me into conversation on public affairs. He is evidently endeavouring to master the great problems of the Empire. He again asked me the same question that he put me at the first private interview that I had last year immediately after his assumption of office, namely, what, in my opinion, were the principal dangers to which the British Power was exposed from the side of the people. He expressed himself so interested in my conversation that he repeatedly asked me to stay and go on, when I asked leave as I found him deeply engaged in writing a quire of foolscap that lay on his table. We of course talked of Lord Cross' Indian Reform Bill. He expressed himself anxious that the Bill might pass, as he was ready to give effect to the new arrangements, and was only afraid lest any extravagant opposition in the Lower House might have the effect of indefinitely postponing a necessary reform.

I do not know whether your Lordship recommended me to Lord Lansdowne, but your Private Secretary in India seemed to have mentioned me, as last year his Lordship spoke of Sir Donald as my friend. At any rate, my personal connection with the head of the Government of India dates from the moment that your Lordship condescended to notice me and make my humble acquaintance at the memorable deputation of Mr. Surendra Nath Banerjee's Indian Association—into which deputation, by the way, I was wheedled under false pretences, for I was no member of that association—a characteristic example of the methods by which our agitators give their movement respectability and weight! For, although I have been long in the Government House List, attending Levées and general parties since I was presented in Lord Lawrence's or Lord Mayo's time, I was too shy to bring myself forward and never got myself specially introduced to the Viceroy, though I heard that my publications—formerly *Mookerjee's Magazine* and latterly *Reis and Rayyet*—were highly spoken of at Government House. The indecent forwardness of my countrymen made me shrink from any appearance of officiousness. Once at an Evening Party, Lord Northbrook was almost thrown against me by the crowd, and he happened—his curiosity probably roused by the turbanned apparition before him—to enquire, and being told I was Mookerjee of *Mookerjee's Magazine*, he warmly shook me by the hand and made many kind enquiries about my publication, which he highly eulogized, and about English literature among the Indians. Soon after I attacked the Baroda Policy of Government in an elaborate pamphlet and I never afterwards went near him.

My friends think me spoiled by European literature in which I believe too much. It is true I have tried to act up to the highest models of conduct, but whatever the complaints of my family and friends at the sacrifices, the ill success in life and even the obloquy this has involved, I strive to be content. If God had taken me in my late illness, I would have gone with the assurance of having given a good example to my countrymen which I hope has not been wholly lost, and which may even be appreciated hereafter.

It must amuse your Lordship to learn the great change in opinion respecting your administration that has occurred and is going on in India since your departure. But I have wearied you much too long for a single letter, and beg to subscribe myself, with great respect,

Yours sincerely,

SAMBHU C. MOOKERJEE.

To Mr. Percy C. Lyon, C.S.

May 17, 1890.

Sir,—I have not the honour of being known to you and consequently hesitate to approach you in a matter pertaining to your Office. But as I have no illegitimate request to make, I have determined, in reliance on your reputation among my countrymen, to risk a forward movement. Without any more beating about the bush, allow me to plunge *in medias res.*

There is just now in the Bengal Office an appeal from a dismissed police officer, one ——, late a Sub-Inspector in the——district.

It appears to me that a poor servant of Government in a difficult line of work has, owing to the weakness of the district administration, been persecuted and victimized at the instance of an influential Vakil party, for the purpose of keeping the Government Pleader in countenance. Any unprejudiced man will see from the papers that there was, from the beginning, no shred of a case against him. The murderer was acquitted by the folly of the Jury. The Sessions Judge fully believed the Sub-Inspector ; he rather blamed the Government Pleader, and that has been the Sub-Inspector's misfortune. There is nothing suspicious in any part of his evidence at any stage of these proceedings, and the officers themselves have been fishing for something plausible to his discredit. He has passed through the fiery ordeal of a criminal prosecution unscathed; his accuser, so to say, himself being the Judge. At last he is ruined by an extra-judicial departmental order.

————is nobody to me. I never knew him before this week. But in my capacity of one of the unpaid advisers of the poor, I have become acquainted with his case. I may be utterly mistaken in my view of it. You will judge for yourself. My object is simply to prevent, if possible, the calamity of the stereotyped office reply that Government sees no reason to interfere. I venture to hope that you will grant the man's case some degree of careful consideration and merciful treatment.

With many apologies for taking up so much of your time,

I beg to subscribe myself,

Sir,

Your most obedient humble servant,

SAMBHU C. MOOKERJEE.

From the Marquis of Dufferin and Ava.

British Embassy,
Rome, May 16, 1890.

My dear Dr. Mookerjee,—I was delighted to get a letter from you, for I am sure you well know that there are very few of my Indian friends towards whom I feel a warmer regard or for whose character and abilities I have greater respect than I have for yours. I am still a diligent reader of "Reis and Rayyet," and in that way I have kept myself pretty well informed of everything that has been going on in India since my departure.

I am, however, very much grieved to learn of your having been so seriously unwell. An attack upon the chest is always a critical matter, and as you are not very robust you must have felt it all the more acutely. Nor does it in the least surprise me that all your friends as well as your readers should have been rendered very anxious about you.

That Lord Lansdowne should like and appreciate you was certain, and I am sure that your admiration for him will increase as you become better acquainted with him.

In regard to my own proceedings I have not much to tell you. We are very pleasantly situated at Rome, which is one of the most interesting capitals of Europe, surrounded by all the most agreeable associations both of Art and Literature, and possessing a very charming station and society. In winter I get some fox-hunting and in the summer boating, which supply the air and exercise necessary for one's health. Rome, however, was not a good place to come to immediately after leaving India, for what is wanted under such circumstances is a bracing climate, which Rome is not. As a consequence I had rather a tiresome though not a really serious illness when I reached London, which was very disappointing as it prevented me from seeing any of my friends. This summer I am going to spend on the sea coast in Italy, so that it will not be until next year that I shall really get my holiday at home.

Believe me, my dear Dr. Mookerjee,

Yours sincerely,

DUFFERIN AND AVA.

To Babu Brahmananda Sinha.

May 23, 1890.

My dear Brahmananda,

I have received no letter from your friend Gunga Prasad. I am glad to think the leader on the Congress Literature and Publisher will do him good, by spreading his name and leading men to do him justice for the great service he has done the cause of the Congress. For my part, I have only made worship to my favourite idol, Justice. Plainly speaking, I love Justice and Truth above everything. It is my delight to do justice and teach men to do likewise. Of course, I desire men to be good, but justice is at the bottom of all goodness. No vulgar, colourless, yielding goodness that is all things to all men, for me ; but a manly sense of the right and becoming, supported by humanity and generosity. Above all, my gospel is that of St. Coleridge—

> He prayeth best, who loveth best
> All things both great and small ;
> For the dear God who loveth us,
> He made and loveth all.

That is superior to anything in the Bible, though of course it springs from, and is a development of, the teaching of the New Testament. It is better than anything in Hindu or even Buddhist scripture. But it is, like Christianity itself, to a great extent, lost on the stern sons of Thor and Woden and their descendants.

It comes home to us of the East.

* * *

The neglect shewn to the memory of poor Robert Knight is most painful to me. I am sorry with a sorrow I can never forget that I was near dying myself when he died, so that I could not perform the last offices of friendship. And now to think that such a man should be quietly ignored by men boasting of patriotism! I have many a time thought of communicating with Narendra Nath Sen, the Ghose brothers and others, or of issuing a circular, but the fear of spoiling the cause has restrained me. I wish to follow, not lead; to do my duty quietly and obscurely without attracting notice. How much noise I might have created from my college days, had I been so disposed! I have not even published as I intended his letters to me, lest I should prejudice my excellent countrymen against a good man for the one sin of loving me.

Homœopathy and Congress are all good

things in their way. But what about your examinations? What are you doing for a profession?

Yours affectionately,
SAMBHU C. MOOKERJEE.

To Miss Ann Marston.

May 27, 1890.

Dear Miss Marston,—Pardon the familiarity of this address. And let me hope that the Gordian knot of difficulty interposed by social customs which, though of great use and importance, are sometimes as irksome and burdensome as unnecessary, may thus be cut, and two human beings situated in two distant countries who cannot well harm one another may possibly, by inter-communication, be rendered the more efficient instruments for doing a little service in God's world. Besides, I would not be regarded as such a stranger. This is not the first occasion of our acquaintance though it be the first of our epistolary correspondence. Although I have not had, and may never have, the honour to be introduced *in propria persona* to you, we have known each other through our common friend Mr. Routledge. For myself, an obscure Brahman on the banks of the Ganges, this acquaintance is not an everyday occurrence. It is indeed a privilege to be thus kindly noticed by a British lady of such rare philanthropy. Pray accept, therefore, my heart's earnest thanks. And for the rest I do pray to the Almighty Father "who made and loveth all" of us, high and low, for your health and happiness and for prosperity to the cause of kindness to the dumb on which you and your associates, of both sexes are embarked.

I would not weaken the solemnity of my feelings at this moment by any more scribbling, but beg to subscribe myself,

With the highest respect,

Dear Madam,

Yours most faithfully,

SAMBHU C. MOOKERJEE.

To the Maharaja of Vizianagram.

June 6, 1890

My dear Maharaja Bahadoor,—I duly received your Highness's telegram and I am truly ashamed to have made so much delay in acknowledging your kindness. But the fact is that my health was again bad and I have only just recovered. This time it was, thank God, no relapse to the terrible chest disease I suffered from at the beginning of the year. It was a low fever accompanied by entire loss of appetite and, above and worst of all, prostration, both physical and mental. I could discover no cause for this sudden attack. I was living with a care for health such as I had never shown, and I was steadily improving and picking up strength, when, without the slightest premonition, this dull fever came on with the attendant symptoms. The heat was great then and some ascribed it to the weather, including my friend and physician Dr. Sircar. But I could not swallow that. My weakness was something of a kind and degree which could not be accounted for by the heat. We are children of the sun and used to his frowns. Whatever the cause, I was truly alarmed, the more so as, though the fever left, the prostration continued. I thought that, even if I lived, I would never recover my strength of body or of mind. When my condition was at its worst it was impossible for me to correct a proof—writing was out of the question. It was with the greatest difficulty that I could finish my work by the evening of Sunday. However, I have gradually got back my appetite and slowly my strength and spirits. What do you think it was? The other day, a clerk who came to see Jogesh Babu, hearing my symptoms, declared it was Influenza. From what he said of that disease I felt inclined to accept his view. I mentioned it to Dr. Sircar, and he too said the same thing, saying he was afraid of alarming me at the time before I had thoroughly recovered from the effects of one serious disease.

I hope Your Highness, Her Highness the good Dowager and, last not least, your own worthy consort are all well. The weather must be pretty hot, and I see that your house at Ooty is being made ready for you.

When does the ceremony of adoption take place?

* * *

God bless you, Maharaja, and preserve you long in health and happiness to do good to your fellowmen and acquire *gyan!*

Yours most faithfully,

SAMBHU C. MOOKERJEE.

To Sir Syed Hasan Ali, Nawab Bahadur.

June 23, 1890.

Your Highness,—I cannot adequately express how shocked I and my family were at the first news of your Highness's illness, and how anxious we have been ever since. I would have written at the time, and might even have gone to Murshidabad, but that we learnt that you had been advised to receive no communications, much less to see any friends. Nor did I write to Mejlah Huzoor or Dewan Fuzl Rubbee, hearing they were entirely occupied with attending upon your Highness. But I made such other enquiries as were open to me. One day I went to Belvedere and enquired of His Honour the Lieutenant-Governor, who told me what he had just heard on Dr. Crombie's return from the Palace. I was much touched by deep and genuine sympathy for your Highness with which Sir Steuart Bayley spoke. His appreciation of your Highness may be seen in the new grand title for which he recommended you and which has been graciously conferred by Her Imperial Majesty, to the joy of your friends and the satisfaction of every one in these three Provinces.

On the 11th Prince Jehan Kadr invited me and Babu Jogesh Chunder Dutt (Manager and Assistant Editor) to the late King's Palace and informed me of the letter he had received under your Highness's own hand. You may imagine with what delight we received this evidence of your recovery.

What shall I say of your kindness, even in your present health, in sending the fruit of the season? I would have immediately acknowledged this token, but that I have been occupied with a vindictive prosecution which had been threatened and has at last been commenced in Court. * * *

I remain, your Highness,

Yours most faithfully,

SAMBHU C. MOOKERJEE.

The prosecution of the editor of *Reis and Rayyet* for defamation is an event in the history of Indian journalism. The time, however, has not yet come when a narrative of its principal incidents can be written from a historian's point of view. That the article which was made the foundation of the charge against the paper was adjudged to be a libel and that Dr. Mookerjee had to apologise for it and unreservedly withdraw, through his counsel, the imputations contained in it, is beside the question. All honest writers when dealing with personalities, must be, more or less, libellous. Take one of the greatest names in modern literature, that of Macaulay. In one sense he was the greatest of "libellers." His word picture of Sir Elijah Impey was deeply resented by his victim's son, an able but long-winded writer, who did his best to rescue his father's memory from the mud thrown on it in the famous essay on Warren Hastings. In his History of England, Macaulay has painted the characters of many statesmen in colour so lurid that, had they been his contemporaries, they would have at once stopped the circulation of the book and lodged its author in jail. Dr. Mookerjee had a philosophical interest in many things of little practical importance. His information may have been often incomplete and even entirely wrong. But his worst enemies could not charge him with acting of malice aforethought. As soon as the article that furnished matter for complaint appeared, a number of people possessed of some influence in native society in Calcutta began to exert themselves most actively in bringing about a criminal prosecution. Some of them were utterly illiterate and incapable of understanding a line that had been written on the subject, yet they proceeded from house to house, exaggerating the manner in which the person referred to in the article had been assailed. Dr. Mookerjee was the sworn foe of humbug and snobbishness. Many who smarted under the chastisement of his caustic pen seized the occasion offered for revenge. And, to the disgrace, be it said, of a section of native society, some who occupied the position of its leaders were actively engaged in promoting the threatened proceedings. Some of his literary brethren whose fame he had assisted in building up at the sacrifice of health and time, were among his secret foes. The prosecution took its course. Those on whose genuine friendship Dr. Mookerjee could rely as on a rock, exerted themselves actively on every side, but in a war of this kind intriguers generally succeed. Proposals were made for a compromise. Dr. Mookerjee was not unwilling to listen to them. But when many hoped and expected that a bad business was about to end, a singular proposition was tacked to the olive branch. It was that Dr. Mookerjee should visit a particular person at his own house. He sturdily declined to do so for reasons which I will not mention here, but which are in no way discreditable to him. The Doctor was advised from the first to fight the case out and offer exculpatory evidence. This he was unwilling to do. He declared that he would rather go to jail than justify what he had written by tendering evidence of its truth ; for the testimony of intimate friends and even of ladies of position might become necessary. A conviction would not pain him more than a charge of breach of confidence based on such a line of defence. Besides, as he had not been actuated by malice, he resolved to consider what he had written in precisely the same light as that on which the nearest relatives of the persons assailed saw it. When they swore that the picture was not true or that its colouring was overcharged, Mookerjee was willing to adopt their views. It was not in his nature to inflict avoidable pain on others. His own relations with the subject of his attack had, at one time, been friendly and even intimate. To offer no defence whatever, he thought was the best course he could follow. He would rather persuade himself that he was in the wrong than permit the raking up of a scandal. The outcome of the case is well known. He offered neither defence nor explanation : and a conviction followed as a matter of course. But the counsel for the prosecution, sympathising with him, said that he felt disinclined to address the Court on the question of punishment. There, he said, stood a literary man of undoubted ability who had for once exceeded the bounds of legitimate criticism. He was willing, under the circumstances, to leave the issue to the unfettered discretion of the Court. The sentence was a fine of Rs. 500.

From Mr. R. D. Mehta.

55, Canning Street,
Calcutta, July 1, 1890.

My dear Fatherly Sambhu Babu,—By the blessing of Great Hormuzd we will be performing one of our sacred services in our new church tomorrow morning, where our Parsee community will congregate, and the service will not end till 10-30; but you can fully rely upon your bad shilling turning up within 11 o'clock. I will make every effort to be at the Police Court as early as possible.

I do sincerely trust and hope that, after your last Saturday's article, the other side will see their way to stop their litigious tendency and will not persevere in their offensive attempt of exhuming the dead.

Be assured that you are uppermost in my thoughts, and we will offer special prayers for you tomorrow for your speedy relief from the present anxious trial.

Believe me,

Ever yours affectionately,

R. D. MEHTA.

Dr. Mookerjee's next correspondent is the son of his old chief, the Nawab Bahadur of Murshidabad, than whom there is no more loyal and enlightened nobleman in "broad Hindustan's dusty meads." At the date of this letter he was slowly recovering from a severe illness.

From Sir Syed Hasan Ali, Nawab Bahadur.

The Palace,

Murshidabad, July 1, 1890.

My dear Sambhu Babu,—I am deeply touched

by your kind letter of the 23rd instant. You have always taken such sincere interest in me and my affairs, that it is no wonder you should feel happy at my joys and be distressed at my sorrows. Please accept my sincerest thanks for your kind sympathy at my unfortunate illness and your good wishes for my recovery, and for your most welcome congratulations on the new mark of distinction that Her Gracious Majesty has been pleased to honour me with, and which, I am sure, I owe, next to the blessings of God, to the kind opinion and good wishes I have the good fortune to enjoy of friends like yourself.

Indeed, it fills up the measure of pride and gratification I felt at the receipt of the honour to know that you are so well pleased with it.

As regards my illness, I am thankful to be able to say that I am much better now and gradually improving. Dr. Meadows is of opinion that if the progress I am making keeps on steadily, there is, if God pleases, every probability of an early restoration of my health.

I am very sorry to hear you have been involved in so serious a case. But I have so much confidence in your ability, experience, prudence and tact, that I don't believe that anything that comes from your pen can be construed into defamation. The charge, I am sure, will fall to the ground and that you will come out with your character thoroughly vindicated, for what you are, a most honourable writer. Hoping to have the pleasure of hearing as much from you soon, I am, with the kindest wishes and regards,

Yours very sincerely,

HASAN ALI MIRZA.

How deeply Dr. Mookerjee was loved by those who had the privilege of knowing him familiarly, will best appear from the following epistle received from an Indian student prosecuting his studies in England. Hundreds of such letters were received by him from persons belonging to all sections of society.

From Mr. J. C. Mookerjee.

Crown Hill Villas,
Harlesden, N. W.
July 18, 1890.

My dear Guruji,—I cannot tell you how shocked I was when I read of your dangerous illness in a recent issue of *Reis and Rayyet.* Allow me to send you my warmest and fondest congratulations on your recovery. Only the very tallest palms—and O Lord! they are few, very few—of dear though desolate Bengal are visible from this distance. What a calamity if any of these be stricken down,—what a landmark lost! Tell the good folk of Baranagore that their thanksgiving was echoed from a solitary room in London where a poor friend of yours in loving fellowship with them went down on his knees too, to be spared, as they are, an almost personal loss.

How is Jogesh Babu and Dr. Sircar? O how

I long to see you all again! But not yet. As I have so much to say and so mùch to do when I go back, my plans are all but immature, my resources all but nil. Mine is yet but the too thin spider's web which I am spinning round about the few stout posts in and near Wellington Square. God give me life and health and strength a few years more, and then back again to my old regiment—back where love directs me, duty strengthens and gratitude cheers!

Affectionately yours,

J. CH. MOOKERJEE.

P. S.—O Sambhu Babu, I could embrace you from this distance. O Lord, to think you are dead!

J. C. M.

From Mr. James Routledge.

Kidwelly, August 21, 1890.

My dear Friend,—I could not get a letter off by the mail of last week, and this week I am somewhat unwell.

I cannot tell you how grateful I am to you for your wonderful notice of my lecture, the kindest and most generous of all notices. My wife was touched by it in a way in which she has not been before for a very long time. We did not expect any notice at the time of your vexatious law case, and in opening the paper it was the law case that was first of all in my mind. We read the notice in silence, taking the paper in turn and we did not say much more during breakfast. We were both deeply affected. Thank you from both our hearts.

We were greatly pained to see the law-suit which must have been one of pure vindictiveness. Your course, I was pleased to find, was calm, considerate and dignified, and though it must have cost you money, that is all you have lost. I shall ask Colonel Burne if he has seen the notice, with its kind reference to himself. Recurring to the suit, I trust your friends will not let you suffer by it. Your words are so wise, so generous, and so adapted to the end in view that to cripple *Reis and Rayyet* would be to injure India's best interests. I am not paying you the least compliment in saying this. I have said it to others in connection with the trial. I am glad to see that my old friend Mr. Wilson is to be photographed. I wish I could have written the biography. I hope he will send me a copy. India has a good friend in Mr. Wilson. I am working very hard, but in four cases out of five for nothing. Two or three days ago an immensely rich man asked me to write a laborious magazine article, and he ended—"I know your interest in the cause, and that we can ask you to do it without offering you any remuneration." I am not quoting the exact words but the meaning. It was a bit laughable coming from a man of money. Still without being asked, I should have done it in defence of the Union. The great comfort is that the works are fast coming to an end and that before long we shall be at rest.

I am, my dear friend, with my wife's and my sincerest regards,

Your firm friend,
JAMES ROUTLEDGE.

To Mr. H. C. Mallik.

August 25, 1890.

My dear Hem Chunder,—Here is your Boswell. It stood me in good stead during the late crisis. Being a handy edition of a whole library of entertaining and instructive reading, I kept it in hand through the sessions as my resource in gaol, should it come to that. I too have a one volume edition, but it is a big tome.

As you do not care for Dowson, send it. I often require to look into it. I am certainly after books of all kinds for something or other; but it is difficult to find books in Calcutta. That article on Cardinal Newman I wrote without referring to a single book, though it has direct and pointed reference to a whole library of volumes. That is a feat of memory of which I am naturally proud. But it is an exceedingly hazardous thing to rely upon such a slippery faculty—particularly at my age and in my weak health. I was apprehensive of committing some fearful blunder—some ludicrous anachronism and so forth. But what could I do? I have not the books. The Dutt Family Library had some, but they are not to be found. You have not got them. There all my resources end. Besides, writing on Sunday evening, any extended search was out of the question. You should buy Newman's *Apologia pro Vitâ suâ.* Do not be frightened at the Latin. The book is all in English and that of the best. If you care for logical exercises or the philosophy of Romanism, his *Grammar of Assent* is the book for you.

Do not forget to send *Eothen.*

Yours affectionately,

SAMBHU C. MOOKERJEE.

To Babu Brahmanand Sinha.

August 27, 1890.

My dear Brahmanand,—Why have I not written to you for so long? The world knows that I have not been sleeping on a bed of roses. And the world knows not of many things I have been suffering from. Yet that is not the true explanation, after all. The world nearer home has wondered at the coolness with which I have taken my prosecution—the shameless efforts of an unexampled conspiracy of all the wealth and influence of native Calcutta assisted by the rabble of your politicians and educated Bengalis to crush *Reis and Rayyet* and its editor to death if possible. Latterly, the enemy could not conceal their mortification that, while they put forth all their activity leaving no stone unturned to attain success in their unholy cause, the object of all their extraordinary attentions preserved an attitude of unconcern. At a time when the whole town was astir, we here pursued the even tenour of our way. People came in numbers, whether as spies or true friends, to hear, and went away as little enlightened as they came. The matter might be discussed downstairs by our own people, but "mum" was the rule in the great Editorial Presence. The two who sit at this table, my friend Jogesh Chunder Dutt, the assistant Editor and Manager of *Reis and Rayyet*, and myself —the two most interested—rarely exchanged views unless once in the course of several days, and that mostly towards the small hours of the night. Not that we did not at all think, but we generally kept our own counsel. That was an example—not simply of courage and steadiness, but also of prudence—which I hope has not been wholly lost on our townsmen. In fact, my whole conduct in regard to the case was an instance of how a grave difficulty and an imminent danger should be met by a man of honour.

You say you have spared your criticism. I

know it, for all that. Your adolescent Lucknow wisdom amounts to this, does it not? that I am an outrageous sinner for not respecting the sanctity of the ashes of departed worth or worthlessness; that at any rate I was not justified in raking up the character of one who was by no means a public man, that I was actuated by malice, that I had a lifelong feud with the deceased, that I was coward enough to wait till he died to attack a man whom I dared not criticize while living, that I had given pain to the surviving family, which I had no business to do, that I was a fool not to retract and apologise when called upon, that I was a greater fool in not submitting to it in the Police Court, and that I have been rightly served in the High Court, &c., &c. Well, you have no reason to be ashamed of these ideas, as you are in a large, and to some extent a good company, in so far as you have the sanction of the Judge. But I am afraid you are all wrong—all of you. You are wrong, too, if you think, as you doubtless do, that the *finale* has been an ignominious defeat for me. You only look to the apparent fact. The conviction and sentence are patent. They were a matter of course. The law is bad. It is a law against truth and the interests of human society, and the High Court interpretation of it is worse. That interpretation was first given in Hearsey's case. * * *

Did you note the terms of Bonnerjee's speech? We maintained the real truth to the last. We never meant to give pain, and expressed our regret for having unwittingly given it. As for the statements, when one of the sons went to the box and denied their truth, all I could do under the circumstances was—always under advice of Counsel—to accept the denial and withdraw the remarks and apologise for them. The thinking part of the public here regard that as a great triumph for me. The Advocate General congratulated me on it, and rebuked the denizens of Asia Minor for their glee at my discomfiture, as they wished to take it. Sir Charles Paul told me that though, in consideration of my poor state of health, he once *wished* the case had ended in the Police Court, though he always said Handley would not dispose of it, yet he was delighted at the result. Had the case not come to the Sessions, I would not have had that opportunity for the kick that I administered to the prosecution through Bonnerjee. So said the Advocate General.

Yours affectionately,
SAMBHU C. MOOKERJEE.

To Mr. Percy C. Lyon, C. S.

August 28, 1890.

Dear Sir,—There was no need for your seeking a precedent for writing to me. Your doing so almost puts me in the wrong, giving my previous communication to you the character of an officious intrusion into official arcana and an impertinence—an act of irreverence—towards one of its ordained ministers. I had no precedent—no pretence whatever for disturbing you, beyond the general right of every man to approach another man, however exalted, in behalf of a brother man in difficulty. I may here as well say, to show how utterly unconnected with me the ex-Police officer is for whom I ventured to trouble you, and indeed how unknown to me, that I never heard what came of his representation, or where he is, or what is he about. I cannot even enquire, having forgotten his name and not knowing the whereabouts of the Brahman (whom I knew only casually) who brought him to me.

It is a great advantage to journalists, who have to perform their difficult duties in haste and without sufficient information, to receive communications from gentlemen like your good self (I use the word "good" not in conventional courtesy, for it was your high reputation—the high terms in which I had heard you spoken of by observers like Nawab Abdool Luteef—that emboldened me to write the first letter I had the honour of addressing you). For myself, I am always open to correction. Although my unfortunate style of writing, I am afraid, prejudices me with hasty readers and those who do not know me, yet I can honestly say I never write from unworthy motives or with any personal views. Mistakes we all are liable to, but I have never hesitated to acknowledge them. My friends even charge me with weakness because of my readiness in this respect.

I am much obliged to you for writing to me as you have done, and truly thankful for your appreciation of my good faith in the paragraph about the death of Mr. Bradford. If any wrong has been done you are quite right in thinking it was perfectly unintentional. It was farthest from my mind to reflect on any person. I aimed at the system. My object, if any, was to suggest a comparison between the Oriental life and the Western. Herein I plead guilty. If anybody thinks that I disparaged the friends and connections of the deceased or imputed to them conscious and special neglect, he does me wrong. I am afraid my words have been taken in a particular sense which they were not intended to convey. The very idea of dying in a hospital is horrible to us, and I meant simply to express that horror. Without imputing blame to any quarter or individual, I only attempted a picture of what is involved in the fact of death in a hospital.

I shall try to explain matters in my next issue. I only regret that the Rev. Chaplain to the Hospital has rushed into print. The interference of the Church militant is not conducive to harmony. Already I see the energy of his vituperation has cowed the poor ——. He will not so easily bully the tiny *Reis*. * * *

And now with a parting apology for the delay of this acknowledgment.

I remain,
Yours sincerely,
SAMBHU C. MOOKERJEE.

To Kumar Kristodas Law.

August 31, 1890.

My dear Kumar,—I am glad you have written and so properly, the more so that it gives me an opportunity of corresponding with you. I took no offence—I am too proud for any petty vanities of that kind—but only smiled. I thought I was not sufficiently known in your house for my voice to be easily recognized in the dark.

Yes, you should have stepped out to see me, for after a man has come all the way from his house to yours he may well expect the rest of his business to be forwarded by you. Besides, take the word of one experienced in books and somewhat in men too—the world is apt to be severe upon the lapses, real or seeming, of the wealthy. As for yourself, your extraordinary prosperity itself provokes so much envy that you have need to be specially careful, if you would be loved and be happy.

You have given a frank and satisfactory explanation, and all I can say is—God bless you and yours.

Believe me to be,
Your sincere *Ashirbadak*,
SAMBHU C. MOOKERJEE.

The first sentence of Sterne's *Sentimental Journey* is "They order this matter better in France." The *Times of India's* London correspondent quoted this sentence wrongly, without, apparently, knowing that he was dealing with a British classic. Dr. Mookerjee, who could not tolerate an inaccurate quotation, noticed it in one of his characteristic paragraphs.

The second sentence relates to a matter of great interest. In a *cause célèbre* at Dacca the daily papers reported Mr. Justice Wilson to have said that in India the giver of a bribe was more to blame than the taker. An article was contributed by Dr. Mookerjee's correspondent in which an extract was made from Macaulay's notes to the Draft Penal Code showing that the opposite view was entertained by its framers. In England givers of bribes are men of education, wealth and influence; takers are ignorant and poor; the motive being generally ambition. In India, the reverse is the case. Givers are poor or at least possessed of no influence; takers are men in power. After the article had been set up in type a reference was made to Mr. M. Ghose as to whether the newspapers had correctly reported Mr. Justice Wilson. Mr. Ghose replied that the reports were all erroneous; and that, as a matter of fact, Mr. Justice Wilson had not said anything that could be construed into a severer condemnation of the giver than the taker of bribes in India. The article appeared in *Reis and Rayyet* with an extract from

Mr. Ghose's letter. As the informant had not been expressly named, Mookerjee's correspondent inquired who the Counsel was who had written in that strain. Was it the Advocate General?

Many of the later translators from Sanskrit have rendered the word *Adhyaya* as "Lesson" and not "Chapter." Dr. Mookerjee subsequently admitted that the former was the more literal translation, though the latter was not incorrect. Babu Kisari Mohan Ganguli pointed out that *Adhyaya* evidently implies so much as can be read at one stretch; and that in ancient India the proper mode of distributing a work would be by *Adhyayas* or lessons. "Chapter" evidently applies to an age of writing and printing. Hence "Lesson" has been adopted by modern scholars and "Chapter" tabooed.

To Babu Kisari Mohan Ganguli.

1, Uckoor Dutt's Lane,
Calcutta, February 18, 1892.

Dear Kisari,—That "the" for "this" in my

mnemonic quotation from Sterne was the veriest slip of heedlessness. Still you have my blessing all the same and my praise all the more. Your letter shows the habits of accuracy in which you have been trained. These are not quite the trifles to be despised that many think them. For one thing, they show the cultivation of learning at first hand. See how the clever literary gossiper of the *Times of India* is at fault in this particular. He has been quoting wrongly a well known passage from a British classic without suspecting it.

My learned friend is neither the Advocate General nor the former Officiating Standing Counsel, who might by this have been Standing Counsel *en permanence*, could he have commanded the patience to wait instead of going over in a huff to the camp of Agitation. Who, then, is the Simon Pure? Try again.

The point in dispute with Sir Henry

Maine was a very simple one. In opposing in the editorial columns of the *Hindoo Patriot* one of the so-called periodical amendments of the Stamp Law—which would be more accurately called periodical enhancements of the Stamp Tax—I happened to cite Bentham as an authority against Judicial Taxation. The Law Member at the next meeting of the Legislative Council had the rashness to rebuke for ignorance those who averred that Bentham was against the Stamp Tax. I retorted in our next issue and was able to turn the tables completely on the great Pandit of the Government of India, quoting chapter and verse, that not only Bentham but the whole school of Utilitarians and philosophers of the *Westminster Review* were opposed to Judicial Taxation.

I send you the first part of Srisa Chandra Basu's *Panini.* You will see that he translates Adhyaya as Chapter. He is not much of an authority, to be sure, but, whatever the etymology, I think that is the ordinary meaning of the word. I am sure you will find "Adhyaya" usually rendered as "Chapter" in accepted translations of Sanskrit works.

I discovered Croker's review of Macaulay, but could not send the book as it was wanted here. Even now for several reasons I cannot send it out. Pray come and read it ; it will not take long. Why not spend a day and even a night too with us ? You will enjoy Croker and the rest.

I am very glad to hear of your boy's examination. God grant that he may pass. This passage of the Rubicon seldom leads to Rome now-a-days. Still there is no living or maintaining caste without accomplishing the feat. There is a meeting of the Senate on Saturday on the late Examination scandal. I am at last one of the Conscript Fathers and have got an invitation. Do you know how your Chief got there ?

I am sorry for your sake for the death of

Guroo Charan's cousin. I can truly sympathize with you, having lost friends myself. There is nothing like friendship for true happiness. Friends cannot be made. They are God's blessings.

Yours always affectionately,
SAMBHU C. MOOKERJEE.

How weak Dr. Mookerjee's health had become in 1892 will appear from the following letter. The slightest exertion fatigued him. He refers to a lecture he delivered on the "Press in India," the preliminary portion of which, treating of the expedients of Hindu and Mussalman rulers for obtaining information as early and in as correct a form as possible, is most interesting. The *Chara* of ancient and mediæval India, and the *Harkara* of the Mussalman epoch were the prototypes of Indian newspapers. The last paragraph refers to the removal of Pandit Ramnath Tarkaratna, after nineteen years of approved service, from his appointment as Travelling Pandit under the Asiatic Society of Bengal. He is one of the soundest of living Sanskrit scholars, but he had incurred the ill-will of many influential Hindus by a disquisition which he had delivered, at the request of Sir A. Croft, K. C. I. E., Director of Public Instruction, in favour of the "Age of Consent Bill." It was a very well reasoned piece of work and completely disposed of the foolish cry that the Hindu religion was at stake when the age of consent was raised from ten to twelve years. The Pandits on the opposition side were all convicted not only of ignorance but of having mutilated texts. Professor Mahes Chandra Nayaratna and Raja Rajendralala Mitra, both of whom were among the adversaries of the Bill, had the magnanimity to forgive his onslaught on their cause. Not so others whose learning should have forbidden them to wreak a cowardly revenge on their staunchest opponent. These combined to effect the ruin of the Pandit. A charge of negligence was brought against him. Sir A. Croft called on him for an explanation, and it was established that the charge was unfounded. Sir Alfred, then President of the Asiatic Society, gave the Pandit a substantial increase of pay. But the former soon afterwards left India and the enemies of the Pandit found it easy enough to work their will. The victim was retried and convicted upon the old and refuted charge, and condemned for neglect of duty, immediately after having been rewarded for diligence. Some strong paragraphs appeared in *Reis and Rayyet*, and the *Statesman* gave a trenchant leader to the subject. The Pandit is venerable by years and character, and his condemnation caused a sensation in the learned world. Dr. Mookerjee felt deeply for the unfortunate scholar. His correspondent was at that time not personally acquainted with the ruined man, but after reading his original Sanskrit poem *Vasudeva Vijayam* he was filled with admiration for his genius. The withdrawal from a fellow creature of his means of subsistence always moved him powerfully.

To Babu Kisari Mohan Ganguli.

June 3, 1892.

Dear Kisari,—We were disappointed at your absence on Wednesday evening. You must have been equally so, I presume. I suppose you got no convenient "conveyancer." Such is the luck of Brahmans!

I was knocked up by my unusual exertions, writing all day from dawn, and then standing reading the writing in a hot and crowded room. I returned prostrated and have not recovered to this moment.

And then here is the heart-rending case of the Pandit of your admiration. It has made me quite miserable. To be done out of one's living after nineteen years' distinguished service for nothing, is no ordinary wrong. My reliance is upon you to save him by your advice and a representation from your tranchant pen.

Yours affectionately,

SAMBHU C. MOOKERJEE.

To Baboo Kali Prosanna Ghosh.

February 27, 1891.

My dear Kali Prosanna Baboo,—Many thanks for your most interesting letters. They are not only welcome as the response of heart to heart—as the unmistakable expression of genuine sympathy in the cause—but valuable as the utterance of a thinker. I am glad to read your account of the interview of my friend Raja Rajendra Narain with the Lieutenant-Governor. The Raja spoke like a man and a true Brahman of the governing class and no scion of a mere priesthood. * * * * As for ourselves, the time is one when every one is bound to declare himself on one side or the other. I can only pity the handful who may have by independent thought come to the conclusion that the Age of Consent Bill interferes with the Hindu religion. Thank God, our religion is more elastic than that! It stands any amount of clipping, especially in its dead twigs and leaves. In the interest of civilization and of our good name as a nation and the credit of our Rishis themselves, every man who pretends to patriotism and culture among us should disavow the tricks of the Garbhadhanists.

It is a great pleasure to know that Dr. Jogender Nath Bhattacharya is appreciated by men like yourself and the Raja. His contribution to the controversy has been very valuable, and remains unanswered.

* * * *

Cheer up, Kali Prosanna Baboo! There is no cause for anxiety. Let us do our duty manfully and we shall beat the barbarians.

They have inflicted irreparable injury on their cause by their unprincipled agitation and, above all, by the puerile demonstration on the maidan of a mob drawn to see the Viceroy and electric light.

Yours truly,

SAMBHU C. MOOKERJEE.

To Kumar (now Raja) Binaya Krishna.

July 2, 1891.

My dear Binaya Kanda,—Yes, that's the name by which I love to call you, and there is no harm in letting you know it.

I was truly shocked to hear of your brother's death. And notwithstanding all that has been reported to me of his misunderstanding in regard to, or his ill-will towards, me, and without thinking him either a philanthropist or a genius, I am sincerely sorry for his loss. He was too young and inexperienced to be a fit object of criticism, while his tastes and pursuits entitled him to a kindly place in the minds of men. We have far too few men of respectable habits and associations to be able to spare one of them.

This judicial strain is not the strain of condolence, perhaps. Nor did I take up my pen to condole with you. Condolence is barred by limitation. That duty belongs to near and dear friends, who have doubtless performed their part. But I cannot, without incurring a charge of cynicism, avoid alluding to this sad bereavement.

My object in writing to you to-day is to make an apology. This morning I accidentally came upon an unopened packet or rather letter of yours written in December. I remember your book because you sent your friend Baboo Gopal Chunder Mookerjee (if I mistake not) to draw my attention to it. He read to me some parts which I pointed out, and I believe I expressed my satisfaction. The letter was not opened and I am guilty of having taken in silence your congratulations on my appointment as an Honorary Magistrate. That, under any circumstances I should not have done. So I beg your pardon. I am touched by your expressions of good will. And, notwithstanding any expressions to the contrary you may have been tempted to make by my support of the Consent Bill, I bless you with all my heart.

I am bound to appreciate your congratulations the more as there are few to pay me that compliment. I am afraid many have taken to heart my unpaid magistracy, though God knows I never applied for it, any more than for the University Fellowship. Perhaps, I ought to tell you that it was the alternative of two titles which were offered to and refused by me.

Yours truly,

SAMBHU C. MOOKERJEE.

To Dr. (now Sir) William H. Rattigan.

July 14, 1891.

My dear Sir,—I was about to write to you on your well-merited elevation to the Supreme Legislative Council, when your note thanking me for the notice in *Reis and Rayyet* came.

Yes, the appointment has been very well received in all quarters. So, sterling merit has still some chance in this world. For you are far from a pushing man, and have never stooped to the arts which bring a man to prominence. It is this that makes the appointment as well as its public reception so agreeable. The Punjab is delighted. The Province is proud of you. The dinner given to you seems to have been a great success. Unfortunately, I have not read the full account of the ceremony, or else I might have noticed it. * * *

I hope in the coming cold weather you will join the Council at Calcutta, and thus give me the opportunity of making your personal acquaintance.

I wonder what you think of the legal aspects of the Manipur business. We certainly want an International Law for India.

What is your opinion of the Native Press? I have just before me, for answering, a long letter received by the last mail from Lord—— which opens with that subject. The writer sat next to Lord Cross who presided at the Newspaper Fund Dinner at which the Secretary of State made the remark which had relieved all connected with native journalism. Lord——says: " I have never seen anything to complain of in the Indian Press published in English."

When will the Warburton *v. The Tribune* litigation come to an end?

At Calcutta, Mr. Handley has sentenced to imprisonment both the proprietor and the publisher of the *Banganibashi.*

Yours truly,

SAMBHU C. MOOKERJEE.

To Rao Bahadur P. Ananda Charlu.

January 28, 1892.

My dear Friend,—Your letter of the 20th instant is most welcome. I am glad to be remembered by you.

* * *

You see that you have applied to the right quarter for information about the great living authority in Hindu Law in Bengal. The Smartha Siromani is my friend and he will be glad to correspond with you on the debatable points and niceties of your common profession. You had better write him as Dr. Jogender Nath Bhattacharya, as Smartha Siromani is a title which he has not adopted as his surname. * * *

On my sick bed I rejoiced to learn that you had taken the chair of President of the last Congress. No better man could have been chosen, and you acquitted yourself nobly in a post of honour and difficulty. Your presidential address is a masterly performance and fully worthy of the accomplished scholar and mature politician that you are. There is not in it the slightest trace of the literary consciousness of the young aspirant which was the only flaw in the otherwise perfect gem of the address of the preceding year. There is only a single word that I regret in so finished a composition—*talented.* I confess I am rather particular. For I see the word used by many able and some even good writers, though as a rule the best writers still avoid it. But that is no objection of any moment, and I would not have mentioned my philological dislike if you were not my friend. * *

Yours sincerely,

SAMBHU C. MOOKERJEE.

Moulvi Syed Mahomed to whom the following letter was addressed, is the son-in-law of an intimate friend, the late Nawab Abdool Luteef Bahadur.

To Moulvi Syed Mahomed.

April 26, 1892.

My dear nephew,—Allow me to congratulate you on the improvement in your composition. You are daily making an advance as a writer in English. Your letters show not only fine natural parts but also a marvellous docility in the use of a most difficult living tongue whose idioms and literary methods are often so very different from our Eastern languages, vernacular or classical. Your energy also is highly creditable to you. I do not wonder that amid the pressure of official work, you find time for writing for self-improvement. For, as I tell my Indian friends who complain of absolute want of leisure for intellectual recreation and literary pursuits, it is those who have least time or opportunity who do most work out of their professional range. The fact is, those who mean to work, do work, making time out of desperate pre-occupation and creating opportunity out of nothing. That is the privilege of the strong man. It is the idle that are always complaining. Many of these poor fellows waste not a few hours in demonstrating their poverty of leisure and proving that they ought not to be expected to fulfil their full share of professional engagements. But though I do not marvel, I cannot help admiring your zeal as well as your skill in compressing so much good work within your limited share of time. I hope you will be able to continue in this way for a due length. For you have just got the opportunity for improvement and are within, but still near, the threshold. You cannot yet stop to take breath for fear of being unconsciously driven back. I have seen some of my Hindu friends, far better equipped educationally than yourself, losing their acquired knack by a few months' holiday, though they gradually picked it up again.

Of late I have conceived a great pride in you. Your docility and industry are most hopeful. But you write too hurriedly. There is no help for it, you have no time to do otherwise. But take care you do not contract a bad literary habit, so that when you have leisure enough you may not still write in haste! We are all slaves of habit. A little more care would improve your composition. There is one common defect in it which jars on my taste since my *Guru* Captain Richardson—the Prince of Poets, critics and literary men in India of his day—warned me at college against it. It is the unnatural order of epithets which he used to characterize as putting the cart before the horse. Thus, it is wrong to say "a grand and beautiful house." It should be "a beautiful and grand" &c. "He is a virtuous and amiable man" may pass, but it would be better as "an amiable and virtuous man." The lesser should precede the greater. Your objections should advance in force not diminish in force as they go along. Of course, I need not tell you that they should not cut each other's throat. But though the principle is a truism, it does not occur to the mind always. Some things do not readily strike us as contradictory. Thus, probably, many writers will not hesitate to say "fine and magnificent," which is nonsense.

Yesterday I met Sir Comer Petheram by appointment. He was to start for Court, so we compressed a world of conversation within twenty minutes. There was occasion to mention your name. When I alluded to your original education in English and how you had picked it up, the Chief listened with rapt attention to my eloquent testimony to your brilliant natural parts, the literary genius of your family and the distinction of your fallen family.

Affectionately yours,
SAMBHU C. MOOKERJEE.

To Mr. K. M. Chatterjee.

April 27, 1892.

My dear Chatto,—That's good of you—to be thankful for a drop. It is English, not Indian. Your Eastern barbarians pass over whole paragraphs and articles as if we were in duty bound to write them up, unless they can complain of some just and necessary qualification to the strain of advocacy or praise. Not so the British. They invariably acknowledge the slightest touch of kindness *en passant.*

In 1890 I received a number of the *Punjab University Magazine* containing a lecture by the Hon'ble Dr. Rattigan on the Greek Tragic Poets. This lecture pleased me much and I reviewed it at length. Rattigan saw it from the publisher of the magazine and wrote to thank the Editor of *Reis* in the most cordial terms, praising the poor little journal highly, and besides sent the Manager a year's subscription. He has been our subscriber ever since, and for little occasional drops like the Lalla Rookhian one which has earned for me your poetical epistle, he always sends thanks which sometimes lead us to wonder what on earth we may have been doing to merit them. Nor is it strangers only that are so particular. It is the rule of European politeness. At the instance of the Viceroy, I was introduced by the Chief Secretary of Bengal to Sir

Edward Bradford when he had chaperoned the late Prince Albert Victor through India and I had a pleasant intercourse with him. Among other things he told me that he had sent to the Queen the Ode to the Prince which we issued at Prinsep's Ghat at H. R. H's landing. He thought highly of the piece and asked me about its authorship, &c. I had no communication with him until one day I received a letter from him thanking me much for the obituary noticc of his son in *Reis and Rayyet*, which, I afterwards learnt, my friend Mr. Wood-Mason had sent him. I have been in constant correspondence with Sir Auckland Colvin since he was Finance Minister. But he does not take remarks about him in *Reis and Rayyet* quite philosophically. He argues with me if they are not to his liking and thanks me when they are in his favour. The other day he acknowledged suitably my comments on a striking speech he delivered at Cawnpur. * *

Yours most faithfully,
SAMBHU C. MOOKERJEE.

From Sir Auckland Colvin.

Government House,
Naini-Tal, May 27, 1892.

My dear Dr. Mookerjee,—I write to thank you for your telegram and, although, as I see you think and as I feel, there is but little to congratulate me on, I appreciate the kindness of your message and admire its epigrammatic form.

The fact is, that after nine years as Councillor and Lieutenant-Governor I do not feel particularly grateful for a decoration which is ordinarily given when a man is appointed (not when he ceases to be) a Lieutenant-Governor.

My reward I look for in the results of my works—the reorganization of the Oudh and Jhansi administration; the reform of the

Police; the water-supply of our five great municipalities; the success against scarcity in Kumaon and Gurhwal in 1890, and again this year; the introduction of technical education, of a measure for Village Munsiffs' Court and Honorary Munsiffs; the great impetus given to vaccination in Municipalities and in the rural tracts; the commencement made in village sanitation; the great and genuine extension of Female Hospitals; the obtaining from India of the two important lines of rail from (a) Lucknow to Benares *viâ* Rai Bareilly, and (b) from Bareilly *viâ* Rampur to Moradabad; the unravelling of the Rampur plot; the action taken in regard to criminal tribes and reformatories; Hume finally buffetted and Wheeler condemned—these things are more satisfaction to me than the stars in many firmaments.

* * *

I was glad to see Mr. Evans knighted,

* * Well! all these are vanities. What is important to us all is health and sufficiency of means. I fear you lack the first, though "Reis and Rayyet" alike contribute to the second. I take both into my retirement, and hope to avail myself of them in some form of literary work. I was born (like you) to write; and by cursed spite only went astray into practical administration.

Yours very sincerely,

A. COLVIN.

To Babu Saradaprasad Banerjee.

Calcutta, December 4, 1892.

My dear Sarada,—It is a bad day, you know, but there is no help for it. Thy will be done!

I am just out of bed to which I went at near three in the morning and then failed to go to sleep from nervous excitement. In fine, the hour is not the best for such references to me.

> "Clamorous Labour with her hundred hands
> Knocks at the golden gate of the morning."

I cannot on the spur of the moment recall where the distich—not line, as you write—occurs. It is familiar verse. It is not in *Locksley Hall*, whether of today or yesterday, having nothing in common with it. It may be in Tennyson for all that—or in Tupper, for anything that I remember just now.

Oonalaska is near Alaska. If that is explaining Hebrew by Ethiopian, then Oonalaska is one of the Aleutian Islands, the chain which all but connects Asia and America.

I can never forget the charming way in which Captain Richardson used to read—

> The wolf's long howl from Oonalaska's shore.

In the stanza you quote from Campbell's "Rainbow," *undeluged earth* certainly means the dry earth after the deluge has been drained off, and the vegetable kingdom, enormously strengthened by the rich silt, quickly, in no time, assuming its green foliage. How, says the Poet, when the Almighty, in pursuance of His covenant with Noah and his progeny and all the creatures who had taken refuge on the ark, displayed the phenomenon of the rainbow, how the reassured patriarchs and progenitors of the denizens of the earth came out of the vessel and landed to bless that holy sign! At first Noah only came out in obedience to the call of God, when He differs made His covenant.

I do not see that your interpretation from mine.

Yours affectionately,
SAMBHU C. MOOKERJEE.

To Babu Nabokissen Ghose.

December 16, 1892.

My dear friend,—The hour is critical, when the country needs the zealous services of all her true sons. At such a time what a pity that such genius as yours should be suppressed by

Fate and forced to inactivity and silence! I see that you have risen in revolt against circumstances and resolutely struck your Vina—the Harp of Hind—with the very best result.

The song—A Lay of Ilium—is spirited and appropriate and altogether remarkably successful, considering the restraints on the Muse of Freedom and War imposed by our political condition. Whatever the serious value of Waller's plea to Charles the Second for the superiority of the Horatian "Ode to Cromwell" over the addresses to the king, there is no doubt that treason is a more efficient inspiration of the Muse than loyalty. Likewise, war is a better stimulus than peace. I marvel how successfully you have overcome the conditions of your effort and given us a Lyric of War—a call to the battle thoroughly consistent with our duty to our sovereign and British rule One passage only—just half a stanza —seems to me open to complaint, or at least liable to misunderstanding. I hope you will alter it. I mean the first half of stanza IV. The tone is exaggerated and enemies may put a serious construction on the lines and the mischievous may make capital of them. Besides, Sir Charles Elliott having allowed jury trial in cases matrimonial, which have hitherto been tried by the Judge only, it seems like a wanton attempt at exaggeration of our grievance to suggest that the honour of our ladies is in danger.

Yours affectionately,
SAMBHU C. MOOKERJEE.

P.S.—I have suggested some variations in the text for whatever they may be worth.

You will be glad to learn, what I have heard just now, that Lord Lansdowne repeatedly said to a friend of mine conversing on the jury agitation that the articles on the subject in *Reis and Rayyet* were very good reading.

S. C. M.

Pandit Ramnath was absent from Calcutta at the time of Professor Deussen's arrival. He was telegraphed to come up at once, as the credit of the Bengal Pandits was at stake. Meanwhile, Mookerjee's correspondent kept the appointment. He took with him Pandit Raj Kumar Nyayaratna of Hatibagan, who was able to improvise good verse in Sanskrit and could speak that language fairly well. Professor Deussen's object in coming to India was to inquire at first hand into the Vedantic philosophy. An interesting conversation took place on the subject of the end attained by Mussalmans who may have died at Benares. If the Hindu scriptures be true, these *mlechchas* must be held to have attained *Nirvana Mukti.* Pandit Rajkumar argued like an orthodox Hindu, maintaining by quotations from the scriptures that it is difficult to ascertain who *really* dies at Benares: for although a man may appear to die there, yet the messengers of Siva generally bear him away to some other place before his death and place an illusory body in the midst of his relatives to deceive them. Pandit Rajkumar was not so good a scholar in Vedanta as in general literature, law and Nyaya, and the Professor's special enquiries had to be reserved. The next day Pandit Ramnath came to Calcutta. The Professor found in him what he desired. His wish to see a Sanskrit play could not be gratified, but through the courtesy of Babu Naba Coomar Raha the Honorary Secretary of the Royal Bengal Theatre, he was shown the mythological play of *Prahlada-charitra.* Mr. H. C. Mallik of Wellington Square got up a party to escort the illustrious guest to the theatre and keep him company there. The Professor was highly gratified with everything he saw and recorded the fact in Sanskrit in the visitors' book. Pandit Ramnath interpreted to him the whole of the play in Sanskrit in a masterly style, reproducing everything of any consequence.

To Babu Kisari Mohan Ganguli.

Calcutta, January 25, 1893.

My dear Kisari,—A German Professor is here, a friend of our nephews the Malliks, who wishes to make the acquaintance of some of our Pandits. He will be at the Malliks' on Friday, the 27th January, at 2 o'clock in the afternoon, when yourself and Pandit Ramnath are invited to meet him. I believe Ramnath speaks Sanskrit, as the Professor is curious to hear the sacred language from the lips of the sacred Aryans of the banks of the Bhagirathi, in the absence of the Brahmans of the Land of the Saraswati and the Drisadwati. At any rate, you will be in attendance to interpret in English. You should be here not later than 1 o'clock.

The stranger is Professor Paul Deussen. He also desires to have the opportunity of seeing some Sanskrit play performed at any of the theatres on Saturday. Could you get up something like it at the Bengal through Naba-coomar Raha? I believe any good mythological play in Bengali would strike a foreigner as a Sanskrit drama. It would be the next best substitute certainly.

Will you make these arrangements and let me know in the evening to-day? Why not come after dark?

Yours affectionately,

SAMBHU C. MOOKERJEE.

The case alluded to in the succeeding letter is one of great interest to students of human nature; and it could have occurred in no country but Bengal. Pandit Ramnath Tarkaratna had published a poem in Sanskrit of 18 cantos entitled *Vasudeva Vijayam.* Its grandeur was such that few could believe that any modern poet had written it; although a critic of acumen would not be imposed upon owing to the abundant references which occur to the inventions of modern science. Some of the Professors of the Sanskrit College, in order to make assurance doubly sure, asked the author to write a canto on the Calcutta International Exhibition which was then (1884) the subject of conversation in society. The author complied with the request. Many of the verses in the first edition were retouched and two entire cantos were added. Enemies were silenced, but the more inveterate among them continued to shake their heads as if in doubt. It was, at last, hinted that the poem was not novel; that at Travancore there existed a manuscript of the same name which corresponded, verse by verse, with the newly published poem. Babu Sib Chandra Guin wrote to the Librarian of the Maharaja of Travancore and, in reply, was told that the "Vasudeva Vijayam" in the Travancore Library was altogether a different work; that it was a grammatical poem of only four cantos and deals with the earlier life of Krishna. A few verses from the manuscript were quoted in proof of this assertion. Thoroughly discomfited in that direction, the conspirators adopted a change of front. A manuscript was forged to show that the published poem corresponded with it. Pandit Ṛamnath, in order to vindicate his reputation, filed a criminal complaint for defamation in the Court of the Presidency Magistrate of Calcutta against one of the supposed detractors. After one adjournment the defendant stated in open court that he had not spoken to any one in disparagement of Pandit Ramnath or in derogation of the originality of his poem. The magistrate, Nawab Syed Ameer Hossein, suggested to Pandit Ramnath that, under the circumstances, he might withdraw his complaint without injury to his reputation. The Pandit replied that his object in taking the proceedings was to force the defendant to produce the much talked of manuscript in court which he would prove to be a forgery. He added that, if the magistrate still thought that he might accept the denial and withdraw the case, he was willing to act in accordance with the suggestion. A few days previously a notice had been served on the defendant calling upon him to produce a manuscript which he was alleged to have shown to others as the original of *Vasudeva Vijayam.* He now denied having spread any evil report touching the complainant, who thereupon withdrew from the prosecution.

The article that appeared in *Reis and Rayyet* was applauded in every quarter as a thoroughly impartial account of this extraordinary quarrel. Dr. Mookerjee, whenever he sought to publish anything upon a question in which his sympathies had been roused on a particular side, always took the greatest care to be impartial.

To Babu Kisari Mohan Ganguli.

February 16, 1893.

Dear Kisari,—Send me an article giving a full account of the Ramnath *vs.* Haraprasad case, from the beginning in chronological order. The tone must be sober and impartial.

The application must stand over for some days at least.

Yours affectionately,

SAMBHU C. MOOKERJEE.

The following letter offers a glimpse into the policy of *Reis and Rayyet* as conducted by Dr. Mookerjee. He never condescended to "puffs." In the present case his correspondent succeeded in convincing him that no advertisement had been intended : that, on the other hand, a truly deserving man, whose acts of piety and public charity had been performed in secrecy and who was of a remarkably unostentatious character, had been sought to be introduced to public notice. Dr. Mookerjee's correspondent himself is equally averse from gratuitous advertisement. The article had only been "glanced over" and the first impression was removed by a careful perusal.

To Babu Kisari Mohan Ganguli.

March 24, 1893.

My dear Kisari,—I have glanced over the first slip of the M.S. enclosed in your note of today. However true, the statement is of the nature of a puff, and all puffs, whatever the claims of their objects or however skilful their authors, degrade a newspaper and seriously hurt it commercially.

Yours affectionately,

SAMBHU C. MOOKERJEE.

After the proceedings in the Calcutta Police Court which ended in an emphatic declaration by the defendant that he had never uttered anything in course of conversation in disparagement of Pandit Ramnath's great work, the latter's enemies began to act with greater caution. The following letter refers to this change of tactics. Pandit Ramnath soon afterwards published a little poem, entitled "Vilápa Lahari" or the "Waves of Lament" which many scholars chose to regard as a finely conceived retaliation. It was a threnody on the death of Naraka, an Asura, or Evil Influence, begotten by Krishna on Mother Earth, whose tyranny grew to such height that Indra induced Krishna to slay him. His mother lamented him long and deeply; but was comforted by her spouse's assurance that Naraka would reappear in the last age; and that the poison of calumny yielded by Old Ocean when churned and held by Mahadeo in his throat would dwell on the lips of her regenerated son. Towards the end occurs a splendid verse, inspired by that in Gray's Elegy beginning "Full many a gem." For the benefit of readers acquainted with Sanskrit I will reproduce it:—

> Adhijalanidhigarbham ratnarájirnikámam
> Sphurati ruchirakantirdhwántadhárántareshu;
> Vikasati maruvátaih çoshanáya prasunam,
> Surabhi nirabhiyuktaprekshanánté vanánté.

The last paragraph of the letter relates to the article headed "The Battle of the Alphabets in Bihar" which appeared in *Reis and Rayyet* of May 27, 1893. It is a powerful attack on the pretentions of Hindi and the Hindi character. It is to be regretted that Government failed to understand the real motive of its advisers who advocated the claims of this alphabet. It was a deliberate and very skilful attempt to repress the Mussalmans of Bihar. The writer, however, omitted one telling argument in support of the Urdu alphabet proving the absurdity of the contention that the Hindi was the national character of Bihar. That argument is founded on the records of the Registration Department. Since its introduction, a small percentage of the documents registered under the law have been in the Hindi character. Is further proof needed to show that Urdu and not Hindi is the true alphabet of the people? Since the taboo laid on Urdu, the Mussulmans in Bihar have been practically shut out from ministerial appointments under Government. The last paragraph of the article condenses a weighty consideration. It runs as follows :—

"The Government are waging a senseless war against history. Their penchant for linguistic purity and loyalty to the alphabet of the gods are a vain effort to go behind the Mahomedan conquest. The rational course is to await the result of popular education. Why force the future?"

To Babu Kisari Mohan Ganguli.

Calcutta, May 30, 1893.

My dear Kisari,—I see that the youngster is still after Pandit Ramnath. Of course, he is incited by bigger people. I think you ought to give a temperate but weighty exposure of his nonsense, pointing out the crime committed by those who are making a cat's paw of this man of straw to satisfy their spite against a gifted contemporary who has achieved the highest laurels in Poesy and Sanskrit learning. You must begin by saying that the Police case has evidently not ended Ramnath's persecution at the hands of his enemies, and close with a suggestion to him to consider whether he should not proceed in a civil way to protect his reputation. If the law is not sufficient to grant that protection it is worth consideration whether the law should not provide for such cases.

Pray let me have a list of the foreign societies and learned men to whom the Mahabharata and Charaka are sent. I have advised Ramnath to send more copies of his poem to Europe and America. Jealousy at home ought to be counteracted by foreign fame, as far as possible.

Have you read the Kaithi leader in the current *Reis?* It traverses debatable ground. I added the concluding paragraph on purpose. What do you think of the rest of the number?

Yours affectionately,

SAMBHU C. MOOKERJEE.

To the Hon'ble A. Sashiah Sastri.

June, 12, 1893.

My dear Sastriji,—It is long, very long since we exchanged words through the post.

But though I do not write, I pray to God to spare you the fullest term of human existence as the most accomplished as well as ablest Indian statesman of the day—one who can be pitted against any Anglo-Indian without fear from the result.

Your young neighbour and caste-fellow Krishnaswami Iyer is here, and not a day passes but we have some talk about you. I have been very much interested in all that I have heard from him. Before this I had known you only superficially—as a master of a pure, nervous style of English and a successful administrator. Now I recognize you as a man of uncommon force of character as well as of native amiability and infinite humour and great versatility and fertility of resources—just the kind of combination that catches my fancy most. I hear that you have the reputation of being the best conversationalist in the South. We badly want such men among us in order to interest Europeans in our weal or woe. They complain that natives have no capacity for conversation. Natives do not eat with Europeans, and if they cannot talk into the bargain, surely all hope of mental intercourse is at an end.

* * *

Believe me, my dear Dewanji,
Yours most sincerely,
SAMBHU C. MOOKERJEE.

To Mr. W. Graham.

June 13, 1893.

Dear Mr. Graham,—You have really been most kind, and I must cry "peccavi" for not having expressed thanks. I say "expressed," for God knows I bless you from the bottom of my soul. Your first letter, at once long and beautiful in sentiment and expression, was a godsend of happiness to me and my entire little camp while we were in the thick of our battle in defence of our right of trial by jury. I not unfrequently receive most encouraging communications from Europe—from literary men, *savants*, members of Parliament, and other men of eminence—but sympathy from Englishmen in India is so rare that your exceptional kindness was peculiarly welcome. Allow me, therefore, to thank you all the more for the first token of your good will in your note of the 7th instant. I would never have known this notice in the *Manchester Guardian*, had you not taken the trouble to send the cutting. It is support to human nature to learn that one's labours not go entirely unnoticed. I perceive that *Reis and Rayyet* has begun to attract attention in England. Lately, one or two Liverpool papers spoke handsomely of it and reproduced an entire article of some length from its columns. I have myself been writing lately of the development of the provincial British Press, but I relied upon my previous knowledge and upon certain general indications. I have no opportunity of seeing the extra-metropolitan journals of the day. The very libraries in this country do not take these in. The great morning papers here doubtless receive some, and perhaps such exclusive institutions as the Bengal Club and your Bar Library.

Yours most truly,

SAMBHU C. MOOKERJEE.

To Babu Jyotish Chunder Banerjee.

June 23, 1893.

My dear Jyotish Chunder,— * * *

You ask me, Whether it is good English to say, "Who is this paper signed by?" or "Who is this card from?" It is English, no doubt, but whether it is good English is the question. I am afraid it will long be a question. These forms of expression are, on the face of them, ungrammatical. How can that be good which is grammatically incorrect? As a matter of fact, however, these forms are in use, in common parlance, not only among the vulgar but also among educated Englishmen. This is another instance of the conflict between English grammar and English usage. And it implies a serious reproach to both the grammarians and the nation. A language is a law to itself. Grammar follows language and not language grammar. They are bad legislators who frame codes so opposed to the manners and instincts of the people that their provisions must be disobeyed at every step. It is due to the incapacity of the grammarians that the English habitually sin against grammar in this particular. People having for ages been wont to say, "Who is this paper signed by?" and "Who is this card from?" it would now sound awkwardly to say "whom" in these queries, and the grammatical speaker would be regarded as a prig or a pedant. But there is no help for it now, I fear. It is too late to change the grammar.

The utmost that may be hoped for is to condone those expressions as colloquialisms. In genuine written composition they will always, as now, be inadmissible. Not all Englishmen of education speak with accuracy, and most of your English in India are not English. So much for the Monghyr pleader's "English gentleman of the station."

Yours affectionately,

SAMBHU C. MOOKERJEE.

P.S.—Are you at Monghyr on service or for a change? Are you staying with Babu Ramlal Mookerjee, Zemindar of Boinchee? If so, will you enquire of him about the early life of the late Raja Degambar Mitter? Babu Ramlal's revered father, the all worthy Thakurdas, knew Mitter well at Berhampur and Cossim-Bazar.

Is there any stir about the coming Bakrid at Monghyr—any quarrel between Shias and Sunnis over *alam* procession and the *tabarra* or anathema pronounced by the Shias against the Sunnis and the Chiefs of their Faith? Any enthusiasm among the Hindus in favour of the Cow Protection movement?

S. C. M.

From Sir Griffith H. P. Evans.

July 1, 1893.

Dear Dr. Sambhu Chunder,—Very many thanks for the two reports. They are both interesting and very different from the mutilated reports in the newspapers. The full account of the debate on the Home Charges is specially valuable. It opens a prospect of our being able to bring such moral pressure to bear through the new Councils and the newspapers on the House of Commons as will secure us some approach to justice as regards the proportion of the English Home charges to be borne by India. It also shows us where to get the information to enable us to discuss the subject. Lord Northbrook's speech and the paper he mentions and particularly the despatch he calls for will place us in a very different position. I could not get the papers as the Government of India is not allowed to publish these matters, and though I knew and stated in my speech that these remonstrances had been neglected and that the India Office was not able to control the charges, yet it was not possible for me to get the papers for the last debate. I thought, however, that I could set the ball rolling and claim the right to discuss these matters, though neither we nor the Government of India have any direct power to settle them. I thought it better to make a start, even with the very imperfect information at my disposal, in the hope of stimulating attention to this matter in England as well as here. The more so as it might be my last chance of speaking in Council, and I know more of what had passed between the Government of India and the Home authorities in former years than any other non-official member. I also know that there had formerly been a doubt as to how far a member of the Indian Legislative Council was in order in discussing matters over which that Council and the Government of India had no control, and I wished to take advantage of the general power to discuss the Budget given by the new Act to assert and exercise that right, which as a practical matter will be a most valuable one in its indirect effects. Lord Cross's speech shews that he appreciates the power thus given to us. It is the want of publicity which has enabled the War Office and the Treasury to have their own way. Had the despatches of the Government of India been published and discussed, these matters would have been forced upon the attention of the House of Commons long ago. But the Government of India is bound to secrecy as to its disputes with the Home authorities, and it is only when the papers are called for by Parliament that they become public property. Even then the Indian Government is bound to bow to orders from England, and it is the non-officials only who can protest, and it is a laborious task for any one to wade through the literature on the subject of Home Charges, the main points of which have been so well summed up by Lord Northbrook.

Many thanks again for thinking of me and sending me the reports. I always read your paper with pleasure, not not only for your clear and incisive style and your humour, but for vigour of your mental grasp and sense of proportion which keeps you from dropping the substance in pursuit of shadows as so many of your countrymen do. You did really valuable work on the Jury question, which has been far too little acknowledged, and I am glad to find it was recognized in the debate.

Yours truly,

G. H. P. EVANS

The enterprise of *Reis and Rayyet* on the mysterious disappearance of the *Sir John Lawrence* with 700 native pilgrims in the Bay of Bengal, had won for that journal the admiration of the *Englishman*, the most enterprising of newspapers in this Presidency. It said that the efforts of *Reis and Rayyet* were not unworthy of a London journal in tracing the names and families of the persons who lost their lives in the ill-fated steamer. The then Law Member of the Viceroy's Council complimented Mookerjee and remarked that *Reis* was the only native paper that stoutly fought for a thorough enquiry into the disaster and for preventive measures against future accidents of the kind.

Dr. Mookerjee's kindness to friends was extraordinary. In fact, it was enough for him to know that any one for whom he had a regard stood in need of money to ensure a prompt and sincere offer of help. Though the first paragraph of the following letter relates to a purely private and personal matter, it is not desirable to suppress it in view of the evidence it affords to establish Dr. Mookerjee's benevolence of disposition.

The remaining portion of the letter furnishes the best explanation of his attitude towards that which was called "The Cow-killing Agitation."

Babu Abala Kanta Sen was the author of certain keys of vernacular school books which the Bengal Government had been obliged to ban, owing to their containing matter which had been pronounced scurrilous. The name "Abala" means "weak!" or "without strength." He had defied the entire Education Department in an article teeming with personal invective. Hence the epithet "redoubtable."

The "dunning letter" from Dr. Mookerjee's correspondent related to a matter which possesses some public interest. Mr. Upendra Nath Das, the eldest son of Babu Srinath Das, an able Vakil of the Calcutta High Court, after a visit to England, attempted to establish a new theatre to be called "Elysium." He applied to Dr. Mookerjee to lend his name to the project. Forthwith it took a definite shape. Many persons of note in Hindu society were induced, in consequence of Dr. Mookerjee's connection with it, to come forward with donations. An advertisement of nearly a column of matter appeared in *Reis and Rayyet* every week. After nearly a year had passed, an article appeared in a now extinct weekly paper charging Mr. U. N. Das with wasting the money collected and doing nothing to inaugurate his theatre. Dr. Mookerjee's correspondent brought the matter to his notice and asked for a letter of introduction to Mr. Das in order to make the necessary enquiries at the fountain-head. The advertisement in *Reis and Rayyet* was discontinued: and with it the project passed into oblivion.

To Babu Kisari Mohan Ganguli.

My dear Kisari,—I am concerned to hear of your anxiety. There is nothing so distracting as anxiety for pence, as I know to my cost, for I have my full share of it. I wish I had received this kind of news from you earlier in the year when I had some money, for then I could have spared what you want. Just now I am in a bad plight.

I am not surprised to see you so exercised.

September 29, 1893.

I was interrupted in the midst of answering your letter on Tuesday. I could not resume the same day, being reminded that it was mail day and that I must in decency write to the good nobleman who sends me, almost weekly, political news from England and whose last three or four letters demanded acknowledgment. The performance of this duty was too much for me in my poor health. In the evening I had fever. In that state, the next day, I was frightened by the apparition of the redoubtle Abala Sen —what a misnomer! On the third day came your "dunning" letter. I am afraid the gods have conspired to drive me mad. For I am almost certain you have taken offence at my ignoring all your several epistles. And today is Friday and not a line for *Reis and Rayyet* ready! I am ill and weak to the last degree. I must therefore be brief.

I enclose the letter you require. I hope it will do. Your tact and Brahman tongue will supply all deficiencies.

With respect to the political topic of your first letter, I was going to say that I was not surprised to see you so affected. You are, dear Kisari, more of a lawyer than a politician, more of a politician than a statesman, just as in literature you are more of a critic than an artist. *Reis and Rayyet* is understood to be conducted by men who live beyond the precincts of courts and jury rooms, men who understand the theory and art of governing. I thought by this you would take care to be mistaken, if necessary, for one of such men.

You seem to have a superstitious dread

of the word *special.* But be at your ease, no special laws have been rushed through the legislature for the destruction of the cow-protectionists. The law was already in existence under which Government are acting; and they will, you may be sure, do nothing which has not been repeatedly done before. And what was the harm in principle or in practice if they did something special in the way of legislation and administration? *Salus republicæ suprema lex.* That is exactly what you lawyers and politicians are apt to forget. I respect law; and justice I reverence above everything, but we should beware of making fetishes of these and paying them blind adoration. Great as law is, my friend, and greater as justice; existence is above them all. You are profoundly ignorant of where you are. You are sleeping in the crater of a volcano. Government have already wasted much valuable time. They listened to your Bengal politicians who would lay the Devil of Discord by holding brotherly meetings of Hindus and Moslems, and so forth. They would not take our stronger counsel; they were afraid of you and your friends—the parliamentary badgers. But their policy of peace-at-any-price only encouraged the spirit of lawlessness, and riot upon riot at last opened their eyes and they decided to act with firmness. The effect cannot now be the same as before, specially if they adopt half measures as if they were

> Willing to wound and yet afraid to strike.

These are difficult matters, and I am not surprised that, in default of special knowledge of the situation, you should be at sea. What surprises me is your talk on the cow-question, your protestation of toleration, &c., &c., all ending in the remark that the riots have been caused by the action of the officials unduly favouring the Mahomedans. But it is useless to argue with one who at this hour says, "a little rowdyism is needed." It is a relief to know that you are no official. But then you would have talked differently—perhaps gone to the other pole. You are still young, Kisari, and it may befit you to be bellicose. I am past the years of recklessness and am for peace. War, even in my time, is not so horrible to contemplate from a safe distance at home. But I have no wit to see the fun of war within my own country and between our own people, and I pray to God to avert such a calamity from us.

I would not part with you in war. If my views seem to you absurd or expressed with rudeness, surely, you may disregard, without serious notice, the observations of a weak old man ill at ease, and still,

Believe me, affectionately yours,

SAMBHU C. MOOKERJEE.

From Colonel Sir J. C. Ardagh.

Viceregal Lodge,

Simla, November 3, 1893.

Dear Dr. Mookerjee,—Extreme pressure of

business has prevented me from answering your letter of the 8th October.

I leave here on the 7th instant with His Excellency for a tour in Burma and we shall arrive in Calcutta on the 13th December.

I shall remain as Private Secretary with Lord Elgin until the end of March. I do not yet know who is to be my successor. I regret that your health debarred you for such a time from personal intercourse with your friends, and I hope I shall see more of you during the ensuing winter.

I am glad to see that you recognise how completely all the measures which have recently been supported by His Excellency are directed towards the real good of the country.

Many of us, yourself among the number, occasionally incur obloquy and unreasonable unpopularity in consequence of our support of a good cause. You mention in your letter the interest excited by the cadastral survey in Bihar, * * *

* * * The matter is one which seems to have excited much animosity and the evidence adduced by the supporters of it seems hardly to have been given its proper weight, while the opponents of it indulge largely in personal abuse.

Many thanks for your suggestion contained in your letter. Trusting to see you thoroughly restored to health on my return,

Believe me, yours sincerely,

J. C. ARDAGH.

The "Sadhus" referred to in the following letter came from Puri (Jagannath) to Dr. Mookerjee's correspondent. There is at Puri a large plot of common land in the vicinity of the temple and over it stood an umbrella-like shade, called Bara-chhata. From time immemorial this plot of land had been occupied by a number of Sadhus, religious mendicants, whose occupation consisted in singing hymns to Lord Jagannath. They were supported by doles from pilgrims visiting the sacred city. The Puri Municipality, under injudicious counsels, resolved to appropriate this plot of ground and eject the holy men. But the citizens supported the Sadhus, and a civil suit was instituted against the Municipality. The Subordinate Judge found for the plaintiffs. The Municipality appealed to the District Judge, who reversed the decision. The Sadhus then preferred a special appeal to the Calcutta High Court. Under the Indian law governing second appeals, the High Court cannot reverse findings of fact arrived at by a lower appellate authority. Dr. Mookerjee always viewed this powerlessness of the High Court as highly illogical. The District Judge differed from the Sub-Judge in his findings of fact, and one would naturally think that, under such circumstances, it would be incumbent upon the second court of appeal to take both findings into consideration. As there was no question of law at stake, the High Court dismissed the appeal, although the Judges gave utterance to an *obiter dictum* to the effect that the Municipality should not have moved in the matter at all. The poor Sadhus, deprived of their ancient rights, sent delegates to Calcutta to move the Government. Mookerjee's correspondent sent them to him with a letter and an article for *Reis and Rayyet* which appeared in due course.

The article on Dr. Rost's retirement appeared in *Reis and Rayyet.* It was much admired both in England and on the continent. Many Oriental scholars shared the sentiments expressed and approved of everything it contained on the enforced retirement of the great Orientalist.

Dr. Rost was profuse in his thanks to Dr. Mookerjee. For no paper in England had noticed the injustice done him and the editor of a famous London daily would not take up the matter, because, as he said, "It is always a losing game to fight the Government."

There was such silence over the action of the India Office, that very few people were aware of it: and one of the ever-watchful friends of India in England did not know that Dr. Rost had ceased to be Librarian till he read the fact in *Reis and Rayyet.* It was months afterwards that the writer on Indian Affairs in the *Times* and one or two other English editors alluded to the subject when speaking of the retirement under the Treasury rules of other Orientalists.

To Babu Kisari Mohan Ganguli.

December 9, 1893.

Dear Kisari,—Between bad health and too much to do with little profit to myself, I could not reply to your previous communications or attend to your several requests, while I hoped to have an early opportunity of explaining matters in person. But you do not come within reach. And now there is another despatch from your good self, for whom I would shed my heart's blood if necessary.

No *Sadhus* have brought your present epistle but a single *murti*, and not much of a personality he, morally or physically, *minus* the turban and the sandal and vermillion paint on the brow! Young in years and simple as a child, he knows nothing about his errand beyond that it is about an umbrella which has been the subject of litigation. His fellow *murti*, who is probably superior to him as a human being and perhaps somewhat of a man of the world, is *non est*, being at his *ásan* at Jagannath Ghat.

Never mind. Whatever these poor asses of faith may be, my Kisari Mohan is all right. So this case will appear in this issue, if possible.

The other subjects you must take up yourself. I am very sorry for Dr. Rost and would do anything for him, but then I am overwhelmed with writing engagements as much as you can be, without the power to do anything beyond polishing up literary matter in the passage through the press.

Just now I cannot lay my hands on the documents you ask which have got embedded into the mass of papers on this table. Besides, it would not be safe to send them by such a messenger as your devotee.

* * *

Yours affectionately,

SAMBHU C. MOOKERJEE.

The succeeding letter has a melancholy interest, as having been among the last penned by the Doctor before his death. The "Bengal" is the famous Theatre of that name in Beadon Street, Calcutta. The article on the Cadastral Survey of Bihar duly appeared in *Reis and Rayyet* and was regarded by many authorities at home and in this country as a complete refutation of the views expressed by Sir A. P. MacDonnell in a minute issued during his term of office as officiating Lieutenant-Governor of Bengal.

To Babu Kisari Mohan Ganguli.

January 12, 1894.

My dear Kisari,—Let me have the books played at the "Bengal."

Never send any notice without the book.

Can you not send tomorrow an article, a short one will do, on the Cadastral Survey? Now that you are well in the midst of the subject, the operation of jotting down a few points must be easy to you.

Yours affectionately,

SAMBHU C. MOOKERJEE.

The last letter Dr. Mookerjee received and which he did not live to acknowledge, was from the Marquis of Lansdowne who had just laid down the office of Viceroy and was returning home.

From the Marquis of Lansdowne.

Hoogly River,

January 27, 1894.

Dear Dr. Mookerjee,—Your kind letter reached me just as I was leaving and I was obliged to write my answer on board the steamer.

* * *

I retain a very agreeable recollection of my intercourse with you during the past five years.

You will receive a copy of my photograph from Colonel Ardagh. With best wishes,

Believe me, dear Dr. Mookerjee,

Yours faithfully,

LANSDOWNE.

LETTERS OF CONDOLENCE.

On the 7th February, 1894, Dr. Mookerjee sank into the "sleep that knows no waking." His death evoked the bitterest sorrow amongst his friends: while thousands to whom he was little more than a name felt instinctively that a great spirit had passed away, who, under happier auspices, might have left a profound mark on the destinies of his country. Let us hope that those whose intrigues and malice had done much to shorten a valuable life were inspired by a becoming remorse for the evil they had wrought. I have decided to print a few of the letters of condolence with which his family and literary associates were honoured.

From H. E. the Earl of Elgin.

Government House,
Calcutta, February 8, 1894.

Dear Sir,—The Viceroy has heard this morning with much regret of the death of Dr. Sambhu Chunder Mookerjee, whose reputation as an able and independent writer was well known to His Excellency, who was looking forward to cultivating his acquaintance. Lord Elgin desires me to communicate an expression of his sympathy to Dr. Mookerjee's family and friends.

I would add my own condolences at the death of my esteemed friend whom I greatly respected, and whose loss I regard as a public one.

I remain, yours very truly,
J. C. Ardagh.

To Baboo Jogesh Chunder Dutt,
Reis and Rayyet.

From Mr. William Graham.

Bar Library,
February 8, 1894.

Dear Babu Jogesh Chunder Dutt,—I am very distressed to hear of the death of Babu Sambhu Chunder this morning. I should have liked to have been able to be present at his cremation last night (if permissible) but surely that is the only way in which one could show one's respect to his memory as a "mlechha."

To Babu Jogesh Ch. Dutt.

From Nawab Syed Ameer Hossein, C.I.E.

Calcutta, February 8, 1894.

My dear Jogesh Babu,—It was with feelings of extreme regret and sorrow that I read in this morning's papers the sad news of the lamented death of my old and respected friend Dr. Mookerjee. In him we have lost a ripe scholar and one of the best writers of the day. I hope you will convey my condolences to the members of his family.

To Babu Jogesh Chunder Dutt.

From Babu Narendra K. Ghose.

February 8, 1894.

My dear Sir,—We are greatly shocked to hear of the sad news. What a loss to us all and to the country! My father (Babu Nabokissen Ghose) is quite upset and is not fit to acknowledge your letter. When he is more composed, he will write to you. With deep sorrow.

To Babu Jogesh Chunder Dutt.

From Mr. O. C. Dutt.

February 8, 1894.

My dear Kisari Babu,—I have just now been shocked to see the announcement of friend Sambhu's death in the *I. D. News.* What a loss! What a terrible loss at this crisis!

To Babu Kisari Mohan Ganguli.

From Moulvi Syed Mahomed Khan Bahadur.

(Telegram.)

Bankipore, February 8, 1894.

Deeply grieved at terrible disaster. Offer sincere condolences.

To Babu Jogesh Chunder Dutt.

The Moulvi followed up the telegram by a letter in which the following passage occurs:—

His death is a great national loss which is simply irreparable. Our community is indeed very unfortunate. It has lost two of its best friends and well-wishers. I have not known any living Hindu who took such great and sincere interest in the cause of Mahomedans and who was so heartily venerated by that community. Dr. Mookerjee's name was a household word in every educated Mahomedan home. My whole family here are in mourning, and their grief could not be greater had they lost a dear and much respected relation.

I wish he could have been spared for a few years more for the good of this country. You know full well that among Mahomedans I am his chief mourner as you must be in your own Hindu community. You had the good fortune to be associated with him for nearly 25 years and you were trained by him to take his place. He made *Reis and Rayyet* a power in the land and it has devolved on you to continue the paper. I sincerely hope you will preserve its integrity and thus immortalise the name of the great philosopher. Your task is most difficult, but God will help you in this great and noble work. I cannot express in words how sincerely and deeply I sympathise with you in this great calamity the brunt of which has fallen upon you; but you must abide by the will of the Almighty Providence and try to keep the memory of the great doctor green.

Kindly convey my most hearty and sincere condolences to his family. May his great soul remain in perpetual peace in heaven!

From the Honorary Secretary, Savitri Library.

Calcutta, February 9, 1894.

Dear Sir,—I beg most respectfully to inform you that the Savitri Library was closed on Thursday and Friday, the 8th and 9th instant, in memory of Dr. Sambhu Chunder Mookerjee who presided at its third anniversary meeting; who was at heart a great well-wisher of the Library; and who in the columns of *Reis and Rayyet* noticed its progress and always encouraged its subscribers with sound advice as to how they should maintain their altogether novel and benevolent instititution. The members of the Library deeply mourn the loss of Dr. Mookerjee whose death they feel as a personal one.

To Babu Jogesh Chunder Dutt,

Reis and Rayyet.

From Moulvi A. K. M. Abdus Subhan.

Chinsura, February 9, 1894.

(Telegram.)

Shocked to hear Dr. Sambhu's sad irreparable death.

To Babu Jogesh Chunder Dutt.

From Rai Bahadur Shib Chunder Banarji.

Bhagalpur, February 9, 1894.

My dear Jogesh Babu,—It has pained me

much to hear of the death of my late lamented friend Dr. Sambhu Chunder Mookerjee. It is a serious loss to the country. We shall miss his writings in *Reis and Rayyet* very much. Kindly convey to his children my deepest sympathy with them at their loss.

To Babu Jogesh Chunder Dutt.

From the Nawab Bahadoor of Murshidabad.

Murshidabad, February 10, 1894.

(Telegram.)

His Highness is very sorry to hear of the death of Dr. Sambhu Chunder Mookerjee and sends his sincerest condolence to the bereaved family.

From Babu Kali Prosanna Ghosh.

Dacca, February 11, 1894.

(Telegram.)

Deeply grieved at the news of sudden death of Dr. Mookerjee. In him Bengal has lost one of her brightest gems. Kindly offer my hearty condolences to the bereaved family and to his friends.

To Babu Jogesh Chunder Dutt.

From Babu Sarat Chunder Roy.

Baloorghat, Dinajpur, Feb. 11, 1894.

My dear Sir,—I am exceedingly grieved to learn that Dr. Sambhu Chunder Mookerjee is no more! One of the greatest of India's sons has passed away from our midst, and his death is an irreparable loss to the country which has been cast into gloom. He was more than a father to me, and in him we have lost our guide, philosopher and friend.

Pray, communicate my heart-felt condolence to the bereaved family of the deceased.

May his soul rest in peace!

To Babu Jogesh Chunder Dutt.

From Mr. A. Krishnasawmy Iyer.

Bombay, February 12, 1894.

My dear Sir,—It is a matter of indescribable sorrow to me that our Doctor should have been cut off so soon. I feel I have lost a father.

To Babu Jogesh Chunder Dutt.

From Baboo Siddheshur Mitter.

February 12, 1894.

My dear Sir,—I have just read in the "Hitabadi" with sorrow I cannot describe, that Dr. Mookerjee is no more. To say that I am overwhelmed with grief would be to give but a meagre account of my feelings at the present moment. I can hardly believe it—it has come upon me so suddenly. When I saw him last in August he was suffering from a bad cold, and was certainly much reduced, but I was not aware of his growing illness, and this sudden announcement comes upon me with redoubled violence.

Elegies and *In Memoriams* will not enhance his worth. Apart from the literary side of his character, his noble heart alone always beating with superhuman love and kindness, would rank him among the princes of men. And how can I ever forget the love and affection that he always bore me!

His death is a loss to the country, a loss to the cause of the advancement of English literature, a loss to the cause of Truth and Independence. It is a loss to the nobler instincts of humanity. I am grieved as I seldom have been.

I trust you will not let the grass grow under your feet before starting some suitable memorial. You must strike while the iron is hot. Bengali energy, Bengali patience, Bengali gratitude, and Bengali grief don't last long.

To Baboo Jogesh Ch. Dutt.

From Sir John Lambert.

February 13, 1894.

Dear Sir,—Will you kindly convey to the family of the late Dr. Sambhu Chunder Mookerjee my deep sympathy at the loss they have sustained?

We shall miss the Doctor's familiar figure and the writings of his facile pen still more.

But I hope that the paper will still flourish, and perpetuate his memory. With compliments.

To Baboo Jogesh Ch. Dutt.

From Babu Dinabandhu Sanyal.

Barakar, February 13, 1894.

Dear Jogesh Babu,—I feel quite upset by the cruelest blow that could have been inflicted on me. The death of my friend Dr. Sambhu Chunder has quite unmanned me, and I feel no relish for my life which seems flat and stale in his absence.

I am suffering from ill health and this bereavement has aggravated my complaint. Hence the delay in conveying my condolence to you and the family.

I know our friend has left many things worth publishing. You are the proper person to edit them with due discretion.

You will be surprised to learn that I had the same disturbed sleep and the same dream (on the night on which Dr. S. died) as Ram Sharma in his "In Memoriam" describes to have been his lot to experience on that fatal night. Strange indeed!

To Babu Jogesh Chunder Dutt.

From H. H. the Maharaja of Vizianagram.

(Telegram.) Madras, February 17, 1895.

Extremely regret the loss irreparable for generations.

To Babu Jogesh Ch. Dutt.

From Babu E. C. Roy.

Bhurtpur, February 17, 1894.

My dear Jogesh Babu,—I learnt with profound sorrow the news of the death of our friend Dr. Sambhu Chunder Mookerjee.

Please convey my sincere condolences to his bereaved family. If there be a movement to erect a memorial, kindly let me know. I will contribute my mite.

In him I have lost a good and kind friend, always ready to help me in my need.

Trust in God and keep up a stout heart in your great sorrow.

To Babu Jogesh Chunder Dutt.

From Babu Prosaddoss Dutt.

"Santibati," Dhoblat, February 17, 1894.

My dear Jogesh Babu,—I cannot adequately

express the heart-felt sorrow I felt on learning the untimely death of dear Sambhu Chunder. You can well understand what it is to be the last survivor of one's best friends who have alas! been carried away prematurely and who were more useful to the world than himself. Kristodas' death was a rude shock to me. In Sambhu Chunder I had still one valued friend left. He, too, is taken away from us! This death again reminds me of the other. In this lonely ocean shore, remote from family and friends, I am dragging my existence racked with a painful disease. My only consolation is that I escape from much unpleasantness which cannot be avoided in Calcutta life. Oh! what a heavy day it is to me. I trust that it will please the Most High to allow my deceased friend's soul rest in peace. I am too much filled with grief to write you more. I have no power to offer due condolence. I am in a position which can be only felt by him who can feel. It is a misfortune to me that I am doomed to mourn my friends whilst I am myself almost on the brink of eternity. I cannot say more.

To Baboo Jogesh Ch. Dutt.

From Babu Surendranath Mookerjee.

February 19, 1894.

My dear Jogesh Babu,—I was laid up with malaria here in Calcutta when the great soul went up to heaven with such brief notice. But, to my misfortune, even this was denied me, for I heard the melancholy news on the third day after he was gone. You must imagine the shock that news gave me, for I have no words to describe it.

* * *

But my own concerns apart *you* can only understand what a loss I have suffered in that of the great life which has thrown you all into such sudden and unspeakable grief. I used to look upon him as my father, and never did I lose a jot of respect and affection which I felt for him from the beginning. Though I have turned a *Sanyasi*, yet I have never forgotten him. I wrote to him from Agra, on first renouncing my former life, that of all things and men, the memory of S. C. M. was the most vivid in my mind. I might forget the world, but not him. I had not seen him for a long time of late, because I was ashamed to shew my face after the failure of the "Sun" which I wanted to make a success first and then see him. But it was, I think, a couple of days before his going on his last journey, that I was thinking of seeing him as soon as I had sufficient strength to do so. But, to my eternal regret, he passed away before that strength came. * * *

Sambhu C. Mookerjee was my *guru*. He made me a literary man and made my reputation as well. * * *

Accept for yourself my heart-felt condolence

for the grief you are now passing through. It is to you the greatest trial in your life. Never did man offer sincerer worship to human worth.

To Babu Jogesh Ch. Dutt.

From Dewan Haridas Viharidas Desai.

Bombay, February 20, 1894.

(Telegram.)

Exceedingly grieved learning premature demise of the learned Doctor. Heartfelt condolences to you all in bereavement.

From Babu Manmatha Nath Banarji.

Seebpore, February, 1894.

My dear Sir,—I am stunned by the news of Dr. Sambhu C. Mookerjee's death. I never heard that he was ailing. The blow must have prostrated you.

Dr. Mookerjee was a prince of men. To know him was to love him and reverence him deeply. The loss the country sustains in his untimely demise is irreparable.

What consolation can be offered to those

who lived in terms of intimacy with Dr. Mookerjee? I can judge of their feelings by my own.

To Babu Kisari Mohan Ganguli.

From Raja Peary Mohan Mookerjee.

Uttarpara, February, 1894.

My dear Sir,—The intelligence of Dr. Sambhu C. Mookerjee's death has come upon us as a stunning blow. He was apparently in good health when I last saw him. The loss to the country is simply irreparable.

To Babu Kisari Mohan Ganguli.

From Babu Manohar Deb.

Bareilly, February 21, 1894.

Dear Sir,—Letters of condolence from unknown and obscure persons are of little moment to the bereaved; nevertheless I cannot but express how deeply I feel the loss of your great friend Babu Sambhu Chunder Mookerjee, of whose death I came to know the other day. For him I entertained the highest esteem. His death has deprived Bengal of the credit hitherto enjoyed by it of possessing the most cultured native of India. I regard him as one of the five truly great men (Pandit Iswar Ch. Vidyasagar, Dr. K. M. Banerjee, Dr. R. L. Mitra, Babus K. C. Sen and Sambhu Ch. Mookerjee) that Bengal has produced in our time, and who gained for Bengal the credit of being the most advanced province in point of education. As they departed from this world, one after the other, their places have not been filled up by equally great successors. With Babu Sambhu C. Mookerjee has passed away the last of these giants, and this is how I regard his death and feel it. His name will, however, survive long after those of the others excepting, perhaps, Dr. Rajendralala Mitra and Iswar Chunder Vidyasagar, are forgotten. But to preserve his memory from oblivion, it is necessary that his writings should be carefully edited just as Landor's writings have been, with such alterations and additions as his hurried writing intended for periodicals may demand. No one is better qualified for this task than yourself, and I hope you will take this hint into consideration. I shall be very glad to subscribe to one copy of this book if it is published.

To Baboo Jogesh Chunder Dutt.

From Mr. R. Belchambers.

February 24, 1894.

My dear Jogesh Chunder,—I was not aware of the serious illness of our friend the late Dr. Sambhu C. Mookerjee. To me, therefore, the announcement of his death was as unexpected, as it was painful. His loss to the public, as a journalist who possessed rare qualifications united to independence of thought, uninfluenced by personal or party feeling, is incalculable, especially at the present time. I deeply commiserate his family, and you also, knowing that you loved him and regarded him as a model of the highest type.

To Baboo Jogesh Ch. Dutt.

From H. H. the Bara Thakur Bahadur, of Hill Tippera.

Agartala, February, 1894.

(Telegram.)

Deeply regret death of Doctor Sambhu Chunder Mookerjee. Convey our sympathy and condolence to the bereaved family.

To Babu Jogesh Chunder Dutt.

From Mr. B. C. Mitra.

Comilla, March 7, 1894.

My dear Jogesh Babu,—I do not know what you have been thinking of me for not adding my name to your list of those who have sent condolences on the death of the greatest Bengali of modern days. I thought that silence was the best expression of deep-felt grief.

To Baboo Jogesh Ch. Dutt.

From Professor A. Vambéry.

Budapest University,
March 6, 1894.

Professor Vambéry begs to express his deeply felt sorrow for the bereavement "Reis and Rayyet" has suffered through the death of Dr. Samhhu Chunder Mookerjee. The deceased was an enlightened and able publicist and his impartiality in questions of religion and nationality might serve as an example to many Christian writers of Europe.

To the editor of "Reis and Rayyet."

The Professor followed up his message of sympathy with the following letter:—

Budapest University,
March 15, 1894.

Dear Sir,—Allow me to express my deeply felt sorrow at the death of Dr. Sambhu Chunder Mookerjee in whom I had come to know and appreciate a writer of rare merits and talents. What particularly struck me was his high-minded toleration towards his Mahomedan countrymen, a virtue which is not too frequently found even here, in Europe, where people are constantly boasting of their enlightened spirit and indulgence towards men of different creed and race. I regret not having had the opportunity of knowing the late Dr. Mookerjee personally, but as a constant reader of his paper it is my agreeable duty to pay to his memory this tribute of respect and admiration.

From Dr. FitzEdward Hall.

Marlesford,

Wickham Market, December 5, 1894.

Dear Sir,—It was with deep regret that I learned of the death of Dr. Sambhu C. Mookerjee. He was not one and twenty when, in company with my revered teacher Iswara Chandra Vidyasagara, I made his acquaintance at the house of my old and lamented friend, Babu Rajinder Dutt. The promise of eminence which he even then gave was amply fulfilled. His example, it is to be hoped, is one that many of his countrymen will emulate. Mr. Skrine's sympathetic memoir of him I trust you will reproduce in its entirety.

To the Editor, *Reis and Rayyet.*

Writing to a correspondent, he again says :—

It grieved me, too, that Dr. Sambhu C. Mookerjee was cut off in the midst of a career of distinguished usefulness. His life, though not long, was a very full one, and his countrymen have lost in him a man of signal ability and sterling worth.

From M. A. Barth.

August 16, 1894.

Dear Sir,—The death of Dr. Sambhu C. Mookerjee was also felt in our part of the world ; not only in England but in France also, among the few who are interested in the course of Hindu opinion and affairs.

To Babu Kisari Mohan Ganguli.

Sir Alfred Croft, Vice-Chancellor, in his address of the year 1895 at the Convocation of the Calcutta University, held on the 26th January, 1895, noticed the death of Dr. Mookerjee in these terms :

"Dr. Sambhu C. Mookerjee's mind was cast in a different mould. Though a staunch

Hindoo he had but little sympathy with the enthusiasts of the Hindoo revival. He held in high respect the strong points of the European character, and he was an indefatigable student of Western literature. At the same time he yielded to none in his admiration for the Eastern world, and in his determination to declare himself, even in the details of his dress, an Oriental. His intimate acquaintance with Mahomedan notabilities in many parts of India gave him a profound sympathy with Mahomedan manners and civilization. It was as journalist that he was best known. His wide reading, his unfailing memory, his extensive travels, his keen appreciation of the humorous, his powers of incisive criticism, gave to his writings a force and an originality such as are rare in journalistic literature. Originality and a wide humanity were, in fact, the leading notes of his remarkable character."

From Mr. James Routledge.

Kidwelly, March 13, 1894.

My dear Sir,—I cannot possibly convey to you a conception of the dismay with which I have read your mournful intelligence of the death of my dear friend Dr. Sambhu Chunder Mookerjee, one of the most loyal-hearted of India's true gentlemen. I was aware that his health had long been in an uncertain state, but that he should die at so early an age never had entered even into my dreams. He was so bright, so genial, so fond of a jest (for or against himself) that I always wrote to him as to one who was destined as a patriarch to take and send down to later times the story of what he and you and I have known in the India of to-day. I wrote to him at times in this strain—"What may not you see long after I have gone for ever from these earthly scenes!" Your letter and copy of the *Reis and Rayyet* almost struck me dumb.

When, however, I had had time to think I reflected that my friend had not lived in vain. He had lived long enough to have shown your countrymen as well as mine, the noble and honourable relations which may exist between them—relations of a generous friendship, cemented by a free expression of opinion on all subjects, and a blessed readiness to believe in each other's sincerity.

And then he was so gentle, so easy to be entreated, so charmingly humorous, and so reluctant to give pain, even where, at times, it was impossible to respect, that I am sure his memory will remain, a thing of life and beauty, long after the elders of this generation —nay, long after the young men of the generation have gone into the silence which no power of man can break. I remember well a little notice which I wrote of his "Travels" and how kindly he acknowledged it. I was about to say that it was not worth acknowledging, but then I should have been wrong. My poor words gave him at least a momentary pleasure—perhaps more—and his gave me a lasting pleasure—one indeed which will not readily pass away.

His loyalty to those who trusted him was at once simple-hearted and superb. The Queen-Empress had not a more loyal subject, or India a truer-hearted son. What splendid duty he did in trying to extinguish race-hatred, you know better than I do, but I too know the fact, and I have often been thankful to God that such a spirit had been given to us to smooth away the littleness, and put aside the self-seeking which mar so many sincere efforts to do good in India.

I am sorry to read that my friend's family are unprovided for, but I am persuaded that the Government will not be remiss in responding to an appeal, which I am sure will be general, in their favour. The sacrifices made by Dr. Mookerjee have been immense, and I think he is of the men whom the sovereign Lady of both lands will delight to honour.

I am a poor man and not likely ever to be a rich one. Had it been in my power, I would have waited for no invitation to do what I would like to recommend to others.

My wife desires to join me in deep sympathy with my (our) friend's family. I always wrote so in his life time and I mournfully do so once again. May the Great Father bless them, and help them to do their duty with their father's example to cheer and lead them on! While they walk in his footsteps they cannot go wrong.

I thank you sincerely for your kind and touching letter. And with kind regards, &c.
To Babu Jogesh Ch. Dutt.

POSTSCRIPT.

I cannot bring this labour of love to a close without acknowledging the obligation under which I have been placed by the spontaneous kindness of other admirers of Mookerjee's character. Babus Kisari Mohan Ganguli, Jogesh Chunder Dutt, P. N. Ker *and* Ramdas Mookerjee *have rendered most willing and effectual help: and but for their devotion I could never have written* finis *to my volume. With all its imperfections I submit it to an indulgent public. If offence be caused by any sins of omission or commission let my critics bear in mind that I have toiled at this record of a noble career amid harassing official cares and in a climate most unfavourable to exercise of my energies. All reasonable cause of complaint shall be removed in a second edition, should one be called for, as it is to be hoped may be the case in the interest of the Doctor's family.*

F. H. S.